People of the
New Testament

Elvis "Raz" Stephens

ISBN: 9798351579887

Victoria Fletcher
hootbookspublishing.biz
vfletcher56@gmail.com

Dedication

This book of poems is dedicated to people who find it interesting to see people of the New Testament talked about in poem form. It does not include them all but it is a fair representation of people written about in this book. It is dedicated to all who want to learn more about the Bible.
I trust you will enjoy it as you read.

Acknowledgments

Miss Victoria Fletcher is my publisher and she does a fine job for me by making sure the book is correctly done and does so in a timely fashion.
These Bible people are an inspiration to me and I find it easy to write about their many and varied activities and teachings in the Bible.
Thank you to the people who read my books and encourage me to keep writing.

Table of Contents

People of the New Testament

Preface Poem

The New Testament is a very enlightening book.
It has lots of great info if we will but take a look.
It tells of Jesus' actions too numerous to mention.
And inside of it, great people draw our attention.

It gives to us what He said and also what He did.
The things He did bless and the things He forbid.
The people who traveled with Him to every place
were greatly amazed by His amazing grace.

The disciples He chose and how He chose them.
Some people's names were changed by Him.
This little book mentions as many as it can.
And how each one fits into His salvation plan.

I learned so much by writing and staying on track.
Making sure to include the very well-known fact
about each of the people that is herein included.
Making sure that nothing was falsely substituted.

As you read these poems, I'm sure you will find
there are lots of things that come to your mind.
Things that you once knew but had slipped away
are brought back to the forefront again today.

So, now take this little book and read it through.
It will re-introduce some of these people to you.
I write these poems for you and your enjoyment.
I trust for you it will be time and money well spent.

I thank each of you greatly, Raz Stephens

Mary, The Virgin Mother of Christ

God loved the world so much He gave His only begotten Son.
We know that the Son must have had an earthly mother.
We learn that God sent an angel to inform young Mary
that of all women on earth, she was chosen above all others.

The Mary of Rome is not the Mary of the Bible.
Catholics are devoted to her and to her they pray.
They say they believe she is the "mother of God."
She is worshiped by them, as if 'God' even yet today.

Mary is, indeed, a woman to be highly honored
by believers in all times and places by me and you.
She's been pronounced "blessed" by the Holy Spirit.
We're not to give her worship but give what is due.

Mary, a young peasant girl in the province of Nazareth,
was of King David's line, through his son Nathan.
She was going about her ordinary life when Gabriel
came to inform her what was now going to be done.

Doubtless, Gabriel looked just like a man to her.
Angels often used this form to reveal themselves to men.
This same angel had come to earth just six months before
to give Zacharias a message that was doubted then.

But now Gabriel had returned to earth once more
and he would tell the young woman why he came.
Thus, Mary met the visitor from another world
and her life would never again be the same.

Mary And The Child

Mary was a godly and a virtuous woman.
We learn she is now with child and still unwed.
The child in her womb has no earthly father.
He was conceived by the Holy Ghost instead.

Mary was engaged to be married to Joseph.
The law was very strict and betrothal now applies.
She was betrothed to Joseph, the town carpenter.
And on this Jewish law, both of them now relies.

This contract could be broken only by adultery.
The engaged couple were virtually man and wife.
They were waiting the year before their marriage.
Being discovered with child, meant danger of her life.

The betrothed must denounce her to the priest.
An investigation must be done and if proof is found,
she must be publicly condemned before them all.
Then to her death she must be stoned to the ground.

This was now the danger that virgin Mary faced.
Mary left and went to Judea, to Elizabeth's there.
She did not go there to hide her condition.
But the wondrous birth with her cousin to share.

After being there three months, she then decided
to go home and tell Joseph what was happening now.
The angel returned once more to assure Joseph.
Then the cloud of doubt was lifted from his brow.

Mary And The Manger

The time had come for the Son of God to be born.
In this world He'd be known as the Son of Man.
He was the Second Person of the Godhead already.
But as the Son of Man, His human life then began.

What a place of all places to begin His earthly life.
No honor guard for Him; He was born in a cattle stall.
Yet there was somehow a little manger they used.
It was a drafty place with straw from wall-to-wall.

What a tragic statement was then to us given.
Yet it is typically tragic in this old world of sin.
It is still today as it was back then, we learn.
Luke says, "There was no room for Him in the inn."

All He was offered at the time when He was born
was a loathsome place that we call a 'cattle shed.'
Here the 'King of kings' and the 'Lord of lords'
at His birth would lay His Godly little head.

That extraordinary Person who lay in that manger
was the long-promised, long-prophesied Son.
He was the long-awaited "Seed of the woman"
whose coming was first told when life had begun.

As Mary now looked at her Son in that manger,
she had no idea that there would be such loss.
He would grow up to become our Savior.
He would die for all mankind's sin on the cross.

Mary And The Christ

Mary must have treasured many memories in her heart.
There were 30 silent years that we do not read about
except when Jesus was 12 years old, and in the temple.
We'd love to hear of those years and remove all doubt.

We would like to know about when He was little.
What did He do back when He was but a teen.
We read about His birth and then about His ministry.
But what did He do and say in the years between.

We find Jesus in attendance at a wedding in Cana.
Mary appealed to Jesus when they had run out of wine.
Jesus told His mother that His time had not yet come.
She referred them to Jesus, all would soon be fine.

Jesus left home when it was time for His ministry.
It was His ministry, His mother had not ought to say.
Soon His accusers said He was violating the Sabbath.
Mary and his brothers came to rescue Him that day.

Three Marys in the New Testament came to Calvary.
His mother, Mary His aunt, and Mary Magdalene.
He clearly saw the problem of His mother being there.
He assigned her care to John, dismissing her from the scene.

Jesus and His mother had a special relationship.
She had to be saved by the Holy Spirit of the Lord.
It is not to mother Mary that we should ever pray.
Mary is to be greatly honored but not to be adored.

Herod

Herod called himself the "Great" thinking it to be true.
He was the most evil of all men living in that day.
He was the king and whatever he said they'd do.
He would do horrible things just to have his way.

He was an Idumean, coming from Edom we learn.
A descendant of Esau, who was Jacob's twin brother.
No love lost between them from the very beginning.
Israel and Edom were always at odds with each other.

There was a silence between the Old and New Testament.
But after 400 years, God was now ready to speak.
He would tell Israel of His miraculous Son's birth.
That they should worship in His birth most unique.

We learn that the Magi came, following the star.
They asked king Herod about the definite sign.
Herod would take desperate steps making sure.
There would be no future king born into this line.

He had their temple rebuilt to win their approval.
Though it cost them many lives doing this task.
Armies of virtual slaves worked day and night.
Doing whatever their slave masters did ask.

The royal maniac drove them with an iron will.
He detested them because he was an Edomite.
His contempt for them was in all he would do.
So, the evil Herod reigned both day and night.

Herod's Dilemma

What a day it must have been when the Magi came asking,
"Where is He that is born King of the Jews?"
The question must have thrown the palace into a quandary.
What would their king say in answer to their views?

They told a strange story of a sovereign and a star.
Herod faced the greatest dilemma of his sinful life.
Yet he pretended that he too wanted to worship the child.
His servants knew there'd be much trouble and strife.

Jesus coming into the world would alter everything.
Herod saw His birth as a challenge to his throne.
He must get rid of this baby somehow and quickly
before His ministry to the Jews could be made known.

Herod would not even settle for the very thought
that a new ruler could possibly take his place.
So, he took steps to eliminate that possibility.
This new born babe he would have to erase.

He gathered the chief priests and scribes together
demanding they tell where the new babe should be.
He did not know his Bible nor did he actually care.
He wanted to assure himself saying he would go see.

Herod's decision was automatic and instinctive.
He gave full reign to his bitter hatred of God's Son.
Telling them to kill all the male babies, making sure.
But the Christ child escaped, taken away on the run.

Herod's Death

Herod's death is scarcely a footnote in the Bible.
Historians tell us it was horrendous no doubt.
He died in agony and in so much horrible pain.
He was eaten by maggots from the inside out.

He had become obese and could hardly walk.
He had lost some teeth and most of his hair.
The dreadful sickness kept him from eating.
He had mortifying wounds, none could compare.

There were sores all over, his stomach was rotten.
His overweight body gave off a horrible smell.
You could not be near him because of the stench.
Looking at him, you knew he was not doing well.

He called for his mercenaries who did his killing.
And said to them, "Go into every city," as he willed,
"And take the leaders of Judaism, put them in jail,
upon the day of my death, they are to be killed."

"Feed them luxuriously and give them comforts.
On the day that I die, you are to kill one and all."
And then he fell back onto his bed, exhausted,
"Go to every city and village, none is too small."

Herod died as he lived— a wicked, ungodly man.
He chose to reject Jesus, God's Son at His birth.
Wise men from the east had come to worship Him.
The question of worship is given to all upon earth.

Joseph

We often hear or tell the story of Christ's birth.
And of how God chose Mary to be His mother.
But we do not spend very much time on Joseph.
Not much time on how they loved one another.

We tell of how that Joseph accepted the fact
that he was to be earthly father to God's Son.
But we only mention him in the overall story
and do not tell of all the good he has done.

Joseph, the village carpenter, it was his work.
He knew what it was like to toil every day.
He does not seem to have very much money.
We know he worked hard for very little pay.

This poor, humble, laboring man stood out.
Though he was not well off, he was very proud.
He had a great ancestry but could only afford
the least expensive sacrifice the law allowed.

Joseph was a direct descendant of King David.
The tools of his trade were a hammer and saw.
He made yokes for oxen, handles for plows,
and doors for houses that left people in awe.

Joseph, following common practice of the time,
brought up his adopted Son into this trade.
He who created galaxies, now uses His hands,
working beside Joseph, His living is made.

Joseph Was Also Called Of God

We know full well the story of Mary,
how God chose her above the rest
of all women living in the world.
It was she who would be the best.

We tend to overlook her husband
betrothed to her though yet unwed.
Joseph was of the lineage of David.
The angel appeared unto him and said,

"Do not fear to take unto thee Mary
for of the Holy Ghost she is conceived."
And Joseph knew it was Father God.
This would be His Son and he believed.

Joseph would offer the child protection
against the evil that King Herod devised.
He took his family and fled into Egypt
as the angel of the Lord that night advised.

Later when King Herod was then dead,
The angel told Joseph to take his wife
and young child with him, going in peace.
They're dead who sought the young child's life.

Joseph proved to be totally yielded
and obedient to all within God's plan.
He was selfless in all of his doings
as the earthly father of the God Man.

Joseph's Engagement

A girl in Nazareth had caught the eye of Joseph.
She was not immaculately conceived as some say.
In the Bible, it does not support any such idea.
She was as good as any young woman in that day.

She was pure, holy, thoughtful, and kind.
God had waited 4,000 years, now He is speaking.
Her personality, character, and her disposition
were exactly what He had all along been seeking.

Young Joseph knew he wanted Mary as his wife.
He felt as many young men feel about 'that one.'
An agreement was formed in presence of witnesses.
The transaction was confirmed, a year must be done.

Imagine Joseph's joy! He was the happiest of men.
She was a princess of the house of David and so
she was kin to Elizabeth and Zacharias the priest.
He'd take her as his wife, he wanted all to know.

This Bible-believing girl was going to marry him.
Heaven above would've appeared a deeper blue.
He sings as he makes his deliveries to people
telling all of his marriage, so everyone knew.

He counts the days and the hours until the event.
He is going to wed Mary and all is now well.
He keeps a lock of her hair under his pillow.
His deep love for her, no rapture can ever tell.

Joseph's Embarrassment

It doesn't take much imagination to picture this scene
of Mary coming into his presence to tell him this.
She said, "I am going to have a baby by the Holy Ghost."
There is no indication he has even given her a kiss.

Joseph is devastated and so absolutely stunned.
"How is this true? Tell me how could this be?"
Knowing he hasn't touched her in a dishonorable way,
she told him she had not committed adultery.

She told Joseph of the way that Elizabeth was now in
and how Zacharias was struck dumb for his doubt.
She said in the same manner I am now with child.
Gabriel, the same angel came and told me about.

How that I would conceive and carry in my womb
the Son of God that I had been chosen to birth.
That I would be overshadowed by the Holy Spirit.
That I was most favored of women upon the earth.

Joseph could not believe that Mary was with child.
He knew she had not been unfaithful to him.
While he thought and pondered on what she said,
she'd go to her cousin's, spending time with them.

Joseph must have questioned in his own mind,
Who would ever believe the story she told?
In the months Mary was gone to Elizabeth's,
Gabriel came to Joseph telling him to be bold.

Joseph's Enlightenment

Soon after Joseph married Mary, there came a decree:
they had to go to where he was born to be enrolled.
It was drawing close to the time of her confinement.
They set out for Bethlehem to do what he was told.

In the providence of God, the decree must be met.
Prophecy said that's where the baby would be born.
This would be at least a hard three-day journey.
The expectant mother was already weary and worn.

Mary was totally exhausted, and Joseph was anxious.
Her time had now come, there was no place to stay.
They'd settle for the night, but the inn had no room.
So, they were directed to a cattle-shed full of hay.

Joseph found a manger and filled it with straw.
The newborn baby would at least have a clean bed.
The Son of God came from the mansions of glory.
From the ivory palaces of heaven to that lowly shed.

We know that the shepherds came, also the Magi.
Joseph moved his family to a much better site.
The angel came again unto Joseph warning him
that Herod sought to destroy baby Jesus outright.

Joseph took his family into Egypt for a while.
When Herod died, the family returned to Palestine.
Joseph wanted to let Jesus grow up in Bethlehem.
God directed him to Nazareth, Jesus would now be fine.

Joseph's Enjoyment

What greater joy could any man on earth have
than being foster father to God's begotten Son.
To watch Jesus grow up and mature into manhood.
Joseph was overly determined to get his job done.

Jesus gave unto Joseph the courtesy of 'father.'
Joseph surrounded Him with the necessities of life.
He made sure that Jesus had every opportunity
and there seemingly came no trouble or strife.

We can imagine Joseph delighted in all Jesus did.
Obeying each and every command with great care.
In school, He must have been such a pleasure.
The other children were happy that He was there.

His enjoyment of the Word of God as He studied
was easily evidenced by the strides He made.
Joseph was proud of his role as earthly father.
Jesus' growth and maturity were equally displayed.

His home was comfortable, small, and primitive.
And very close by was Joseph's carpenter shop.
They worked together on a lot of projects.
Jesus' questions to Joseph seemed never to stop.

Joseph enjoyed his part as protector and provider.
He made sure all that was done had Jesus in it.
Knowing one day Jesus would have His ministry.
For now, Joseph no doubt enjoyed every minute.

The Leper and His Cry

"Leper." The very word sent tingles down the spine.
It summed up as horrible, tragic, and disgusting, too.
Leprosy was a living death for those who had it.
It was most fearful to any well-meaning Jew.

They were terrified of it. It was the 'stroke of God.'
They thought anyone having it was under God's curse.
The law of Moses legislated against all who had it
to stay away from others to not make things worse.

Obliged by the law, they kept their mouth covered.
When approached, they would cry out, "UNCLEAN!"
Leprosy was regarded as different in degree and kind.
For one to be kind to a Leper was hardly ever seen.

Leprosy was foul and contaminating and vile.
That's evident with the way the Holy Spirit records.
With sick people in general and lepers specifically.
The sick were healed and the leper came to the Lord.

He was a leper. That is all we know about him.
We have no idea about his name nor how old.
If he was married with a wife and family, or single.
We only know that this day, he became bold.

The fact he was a leper, gave unto him no hope.
There was no cure; there was no use in his trying.
He lived a poor existence, separated from others.
He knew that soon, he would also be dying.

The Leper's Misery

We do not know where he came from that day,
whether he came from a big city or a small.
We do know that he was a leper in misery.
That one fact being a leper outstood them all.

We know that leprosy was a sentence of death.
People who had it knew they had nothing to gain.
It was contagious to any who came into contact.
The discharges from sores kept the leper in pain.

The leper approached Christ and cried "UNCLEAN!"
What a horrible picture of decomposition and decay.
His touch was contamination to any one too near.
They had excommunicated him to keep him away.

Lepers oft used their condition to terrorize others
who would be fearful and give in to demands.
But this leper was different, he wanted to see Jesus.
He had expressed interest in His laying on of hands.

It is not at all surprising, that throughout the Bible,
leprosy is a type and a picture of man's sin.
It acts on the body as sin does on man's soul.
They try to hide the fact but it shows up again.

As he came toward Jesus, he did not have to call.
Jesus saw that he was laden down head to toe.
But Jesus took compassion, before his "UNCLEAN!"
Jesus would now heal him, and then let him go.

The Leper's Marvelous Healing

He had heard about Jesus who came to Capernaum
and took up residence among the people there.
People flocked from all over to hear His teaching.
He astonished them with His miracles of great care.

There seemed to be no one that this young prophet
could not heal of any illness or any disease known.
And so, he came trusting he would be made clean.
This young Miracle Worker was a prophet of His own.

He knew Jesus could, if only Jesus would do it.
"Lord, if Thou wilt, Thou can make me clean."
He did not question, that would show unbelief.
His faith in Jesus as healer could easily be seen.

To come as he did, he had to put away all doubt.
It took great courage in this great a crowd.
But he wanted Jesus to hear and see him.
So "UNCLEAN! Unclean!" he cried very loud.

I am sure all the others were actually hostile.
How dare he come into their midst this way?
Daring to defy all the written taboos and laws.
He had to see Jesus and it must be today.

Jesus had no fear of contamination from him.
He simply spoke saying, "I will, be thou clean."
As soon as He spoke, the leprosy departed.
Such marvelous conversion had never been seen.

The Leper's Mistaken Confession

Now that the leper is healed, he must now go
to the priest nearby and there he must show.
Ordinarily, Jesus would want him to stay.
With leprosy now gone, it'd be different today.

Jesus straitly charged him, "You're to tell no one."
But he couldn't keep secret the thing that was done.
"Go show the priest, as Moses did command."
But he wanted to show everyone on hand.

The priests needed to see that Jesus obeyed.
He sent the leper there to help and persuade.
Jesus had as much love for the priest as He did.
For the soul of the leper who had to stay hid.

Now he tells him to go and show himself there.
Witnessing that He had done this with care.
But the leper went out and published it much.
How he was cleansed by Jesus' one touch.

The man who had to cry "Unclean" out loud,
now had his healing and also a big crowd.
Jesus had no need for huge crowds that day.
They hindered His work and got in His way.

It would've been better had he done as told.
But the cleansed leper was now being bold.
When Jesus tells you what you are to do,
His love, and mercy, will see you through.

Simeon

Simeon was a man that we know not much about.
He appears for a moment with a job no doubt.
We know he was very old, the Bible does say.
He stayed there in the temple most every day.

Simeon listened to that 'still small voice'
knowing one day, he would be able to rejoice.
He'd see Jesus when they first brought Him in.
The Baby who would grow to save us from sin.

Simeon knew in his lifetime Jesus he would see.
So he waited, and each day in the temple he'd be.
When Mary and Joseph brought Jesus and came.
He knew immediately Jesus was one and the same.

Simeon is recorded as having a hand in the Book.
He held Jesus in his arms and took a long look.
He'd waited for 'the consolation of Israel' and now
he knew the Bible by heart. He'd see Jesus somehow.

There was no one close by who seemed to care
that the newborn Christ-child was even there.
There were thousands of priests, too many indeed.
But none of them could see their own need.

Old Simeon had nothing in common with these.
Taking people's money and did what they'd please.
Simeon was promised death wouldn't come his way.
He said, "Mine eyes have seen Thy salvation today."
The Holy Spirit had told him he'd see Jesus one day.

Anna

Anna, an old woman, widowed eighty-four years now.
Once married for seven years, continues on somehow.
She loved God and followed Him and we are told
that here she is now well over a hundred years old.

Anna was humble and happy, full of godlike grace.
She had grown old in godliness, here in this place.
Her name is recorded in this most sacred text.
The Lord Jesus Christ, she wanted to see next.

When Mary and Joseph brought Jesus there to obey
and to pay their sacrifice for the boy-child that day,
God allowed Anna to hold him and soon she did so.
He was born to save others and this she did know.

Anna could've been bitter when her husband died.
She could have blamed God and yet she relied.
She could've turned into a sour old woman then
and missed holding the One who saves from sin.

She found a quiet corner and made there her home.
Each day in the temple and the days yet to come.
Into the women's court was as far as she got.
Luke says, "And from the temple she departed not."

She determined to be happy, in the temple she'd live
and give her service to God, whatever she could give.
She knew what she was doing, though misunderstood.
She dedicated herself to God in her long widowhood.

Anna Gives Praise

Anna's chief delight seemed to be where people came.
She enjoyed seeing them coming to call on His name.
In the temple of the Lord is where she wanted to be.
She often said, "When He comes, there He will find me."

Under the Jewish law, a widow could not dispose
her property and the rabbis took advantage of those.
Anna had not let their hypocrisy rob her of her joy.
Now she lives in the temple and awaits seeing the boy.

Her whole life revolved around the temple today.
A verse in her Bible said He would come that way.
She triumphed over all excuses people then made.
Her excitement and anxiousness would never fade.

Serving God, "with prayer and fasting by night and day."
Her life's work was to praise the Lord and to pray.
She has a vision that one day she will see Him.
So she waits, and she sees people, but so far not them.

Anna notices a man and a woman enter the court
with a baby wrapped in a blanket. They are of poor sort.
Anna sees Simeon approach them there and then.
She knew immediately it was the Savior of men.

Anna's heart leaps, knowing the Savior has been born.
She knows lots of people and promises to warn.
Anna then bursts into thanksgiving and praise.
Giving testimony of God's faithfulness always.

John The Baptist

John was older than Jesus by only three months.
Elizabeth, a cousin to Mary, was John's mother.
John came from the family of Aaron the priest
who served as priests to guide one another.

The priesthood was not an open profession.
Open to anyone who wanted that claim.
It was only fitting for those descendants of Levi.
John certainly had that background in his name.

But John chose a completely different pathway.
He decided another prophet was what Israel needed.
So, John turned his back on a secure profession,
headed off into the wilderness. God had interceded.

We do not know how old he was, nor how long
he ventured into the wilderness preparing to preach.
We know from his birth he was set aside a Nazarite.
One of only three Nazarites the Bible did beseech.

John was set aside to live his life only for God.
He was filled with the Holy Ghost from his birth.
His parents being Hebrew, taught him about God.
His life was something very rare in the wide earth.

What a man was John! He stood up to Herod,
denounced him publicly, enduring Herodias' rage.
John was willing to fade into the background
when Jesus came forth to occupy life's stage.

John The Man

John shook his nation to its foundations.
Jesus said John was the greatest man ever born.
He came forth preaching, out of the wilderness.
In those days of preaching, he began to forewarn.

The preaching of John the Baptist was well hated.
His advent marked the beginning of a new day.
John trolled the bell over the decadent age.
Pealing out of a new beginning in a new way.

He stayed in the wilderness for a good while
praying, fasting, and preaching to them.
He waited on God to make His move.
John didn't go to the crowds, they came to him.

It was estimated that, from start to finish,
there were about a million who had come to hear
John preach his message there in the wilderness.
This desert preacher made his message so clear.

John's pulpit was most likely a rocky ledge
that he stood on and spoke to them loud.
He preached that there was a Man coming.
He delivered his message to a collected crowd.

What a place this was to begin his preaching.
Laboring with no complaint, this was his sphere.
John was ever faithful to his Godly calling.
Telling them that the Lamb of God was now here.

John's Style of Life

John did not beat around the bush with men.
He would thoroughly thrash them for their sin.
He went straight for the juggler and would say,
"Repent! Repent! You must repent today."

The Holy Spirit's great appeal, after all,
is to anyone who will listen to His call.
The Holy Spirit speaks to us not by chance.
He knows our entire being, our circumstance.

John's lifestyle, wedded to his personality,
gave unto his preaching devastating authority.
He ate course food and was often known to fast.
People listened to him, weeping over their past.

The crowds came to John wherever he then went.
And he led many of them with his call to repent.
All would be aware that Christ was on His way.
That they could be delivered from all sin today.

People flocked to John, wanting to hear him preach.
The old, the young, the rich, and the poor he did beseech.
Some came because they were burdened by their sin.
Others came curiously to see who was being brought in.

John did not make repentance easy to obtain.
His altar call was calculated to strike out every stain.
"Repent! Come into the water just as you are dressed."
Those who asked forgiveness, he with baptism blessed.

John Had Critics

No matter how popular John had become,
all preachers have critics and John had some.
They dismissed John and the message he brought.
They didn't believe judgment would be brought.

They said, "We are children of Abraham by birth."
They didn't believe a Savior was coming to earth.
John's critics came mostly from the religious crowd.
Yet the outcast sinners came not being at all proud.

John was a God-sent forerunner, a herald we read.
Commissioned from on high to awaken their need.
He spoke scathingly to those he knew would reject.
He called for sinful men to repent and reflect.

John exposed the leaders' conduct and their conceit.
"O generation of vipers," you are not ready to meet.
You are sons of serpents who will not accept Him.
We couldn't get away with how John spoke to them.

The leaders needed repentance just as any in the land.
John offered to them the answer, the Christ at hand.
Their lives were very shallow, empty, and a sham.
They accepted not his teaching of the great I AM.

They rejected both John and the Christ he preached.
They continued in sin and would not be reached.
John said as a tree they would soon be hewn down.
Today we know John the Baptist was a man of renown.

Herod Agrippa I

Herod Agrippa I grabbed the helm of the Jewish state
with a murderous hand and a whole lot of hate.
The Herods were a bad lot, true children of Esau.
With bloody hands, they're as bad as you ever saw.

They were completely lawless and kept people worried.
You'd trust a rattlesnake better than you could a Herod.
Woe would betide a man who crossed one of them.
Herod would soon take all he wanted away from him.

Herod Agrippa I, the man in the book of Acts we meet.
Not Herod who murdered John, bringing him to defeat.
Thinking they were big, always splashing their weight.
Herod Agrippa I was the grandson of Herod the Great.

The father of Agrippa I was Aristobulus, by name.
The son of Herod the Great, but soldiers one day came
and murdered his father by his grandfather's command.
Agrippa I was sent by his mother into another land.

There was a lot of intermarrying among the family then.
There was no mystery that they all ended up being kin.
The Herods were unscrupulous and that was well known.
The only law they followed was a law of their own.

Herod Agrippa I came back to Palestine wearing a crown.
But the Jewish people didn't respect this man of renown.
He tried to make friends among them when he could.
But the Jews did not trust him and they never would.

Herod Agrippa's Hideous Crime

The friends of the Sanhedrin became more infuriated
at those who became Christians, their hatred is stated.
Herod Agrippa I knew he must be a Sanhedrin fiend.
And try to bring this fishermen's movement to an end.

How complete was their indifference to a Jewish threat.
King Herod Agrippa I knew it would get much worse yet.
He put it all together and soon came up with a hunch.
The leaders must die; he would kill off the whole bunch.

He came up with a plan that followed his aims.
The first one he murdered was the disciple James.
James and John had left fishing at Jesus' first call.
They became intimate disciples giving up all.

James was one who was to watch and to pray
and wait upon Jesus in Gethsemane's garden that day.
James was a great speaker, and many wanted to hear.
That caused Herod Agrippa I to have very much fear.

James went quietly about telling all of his story
about Jesus who had come down from His glory.
Inviting them into the church that was now started,
Jesus would receive those who from sin departed.

James was the first martyr of the apostle band.
Agrippa was threatened and had James taken in hand.
He ordered James executed for this very cause.
Then he sat back receiving much approval and applause.

Agrippa's Detention of Peter

Agrippa saw that the death of James pleased the Jews.
He proceeded to take Apostle Peter into detention.
It was on the anniversary of the murder of Christ.
Agrippa's new friends were giving him much attention.

Herod had Peter taken and put immediately in chains.
His death sentence signed, to be carried out the next day.
You'd think Peter would fret and worry all night.
But Peter went fast asleep, knowing the church would pray.

Peter's angel came at night right into his guarded cell.
Roman custom had it that he was chained between two.
Peter must have thought that he was only dreaming
when the angel awakened him, "I have come for you."

Prayer was being made without ceasing for Peter.
The church needed him, and they prayed he'd be set free.
On the surface it seemed Herod Agrippa had won.
Peter, now free, went to Mary's house to let them all see.

Herod went back to Caesarea and there he abode.
Another crisis arose that he chose to take into hand.
A delegation came to offer him peace and surrender.
He dressed in a blazing robe that made him look grand.

In the bright sunlight, his robe blazed and flashed.
They cried out, "That is God." He accepted their praise.
The watching angel smote him during his adulation.
King Herod Agrippa I suffered and died in only five days.

Apostle Peter

The Bible gives us several candid pictures of Simon Peter:
impulsive, apolitical, impressionable, always being direct.
He said what he meant and meant what he said directly.
His straight forwardness was always very easy to detect.

He had a brother, the very best kind of brother there is.
He was not like Simon, but he had some fervor and fire.
His name was Andrew, a disciple of John the Baptist.
Learning about the kingdom of God was his desire.

One day he came to Simon and excitedly told him,
"We have found the Christ. The Son of God I have met.
Andrew insisted that Simon come and meet Jesus.
Simon soon agreed and the two off together then set.

Jesus said, "Hello Simon, I'm going to call you Peter."
"There is a rock-like quality about you that I can use."
That is our very first snapshot of Peter and the Lord.
Peter had no idea of their coming suffering and abuse.

Jesus wanted both Andrew and Peter to follow Him,
to become a major part of His new disciple band.
It would be tough, and He chose some tough men
to come and travel with Him throughout the land.

Apostle Peter would go down in Bible history
as being a great man for mostly doing Christ's will.
He would go on to preach and teach of salvation.
At Peter's death, Jesus said, "Come, be with Me still."

Peter and The Storm

Jesus had preached to an enormous crowd today.
He had taught that His kingdom was on its way.
It was an exciting day for every one of them.
Just to one of His disciples and listen to Him.

They had fed five thousand plus with just a lunch.
Peter saw the barley loaves and he had a hunch.
The two small fishes would also help fill the need.
Jesus would multiply those, the people He'd feed.

Peter distributed his basket full to that big crowd.
What a miraculous blessing that day was allowed.
Peter gave food out and quickly came back for more.
At the end of the banquet, twelve baskets were left o'er.

The people wanted to make Jesus king that very day.
But He refused them, however, and sent them away.
Jesus told His disciples to get into the boat and ride.
And He would soon see them on the other side.

Halfway across the lake, Peter knew it was not norm.
There'd suddenly come up a very boisterous storm.
The winds howled, the waves heaved, causing unrest.
The disciples struggled against the terrible tempest.

Then they saw Jesus, walking on the water— a shape.
It must be a ghost, there's nowhere to escape.
Jesus said to Peter, "Be not afraid. Come. It is I."
When Peter looked to the Lord, he didn't have to die.

Peter With Tears in His Eyes

The shadow of the cross was dark and impending.
Peter's daily access to Jesus would soon be ending.
Jesus warned people would smite Him and He would die.
But Peter said, "Others may offend You. Certainly not I."

"You think so Peter?" Jesus gave Peter some advice.
"Before the cock crows, you will deny Me thrice."
The Jews bullied and beat Jesus to their desire.
And Peter just sat warming himself by the fire.

Yet Peter did deny Him, each time being worse.
The last of the three was with an oath and a curse.
Then the cock crowed. He intercepted Jesus' look
of love and forgiveness. He wasn't being forsook.

Never had Peter experienced a darker night.
He was so ashamed, so sorry, he had not done right.
In his mind he heard Jesus' words then repeat,
"Satan wants to have you, to sift you like wheat."

"But I have prayed for thee." What a wonderful prayer.
Peter certainly would need that this very same hour.
Had not Jesus looked at him in forgiveness just now,
Peter just may have done what Judas did somehow.

We read that Peter went out and he bitterly wept.
On the path of sanity yet with deep sorrow he kept.
We find Peter later following Jesus' commands.
He received full absolution at Jesus' pierced hands.

Peter Goes Fishing

Peter, at the death of Jesus, had become defeated.
The words Jesus told him in his mind were repeated.
Jesus told him He would meet him back in Galilee.
So, Peter knew that was the place he needed to be.

Peter had become discouraged, somewhat subdued.
He needed his confidence and hope be renewed.
So, then off to his familiar surroundings he went.
Back to where his time with fishing was spent.

Peter soon began to feel like himself once more.
Some other disciples helped push from the shore.
They would fish all night and have nothing to show.
An effort they put into making Peter's fishing go.

Peter's fishing expedition wasn't so good after all.
Years ago he had left that to answer Jesus' call.
Jesus had called him to become a fisher of men.
Why would he try to go back to fishing again?

As they came back to land without filling their desire,
they got close enough to see a man tending a fire.
He said to Peter, "Cast your net on the other side."
They caught so many fish, the net could hardly provide.

Jesus was there on land, cooking bread and fish.
The disciples sat down, ate as much as they could wish.
Jesus picked out Peter, asking him, "Do you love Me?"
"I called you out of fishing my shepherd/pastor to be."

Peter With Pen in Hand

It is likely that Peter came to regret his slow start.
But he has no problem sharing with people his heart.
Others had taken early initiative and had moved on.
The Spirit was now spread but it was not at all gone.

Paul had blazed the trail to the many regions beyond.
He had gone across Roman Asia, as it is well known.
Yet Peter was a latecomer in accepting the Gentile.
He would also become their champion in a while.

The climate changed and Rome had stirred in anger.
It came against the church, putting them in danger.
Peter thinks of Gentile churches spread far and wide.
They are now dear to his heart, he wants to provide.

He thinks, too, of the Jewish Christians. He will begin
to write to them all, so he now picks up his pen.
He will write two letters that leaves us no doubt.
One of trouble within, the other of trouble without.

His 1st letter was to the suffering church under attack.
His 2nd the seduced church's apostasy, what they lacked.
Peter enjoyed the goodwill of the churches everywhere.
A letter from him would surely create quite a stir.

We do not think of Peter very much as a writer.
He was more of an impulsive man, an exciter.
Peter wrote the truth about what was required.
We know that his letters were divinely inspired.

Peter Has Empty Pockets

We find Peter and John once again on their way,
headed to the temple. It is again time to pray.
There were lots of people that surrounded them
living in this busy, impersonal city of Jerusalem.

People still came to the temple. It was obsolete.
Habit drew them back, making them feel complete.
The temple atmosphere had them much charged.
The embellished court they did not much regard.

Gentiles were allowed into the court with their name.
Jews could go further when to the temple they came.
The "holy of holies" occupied the holy center place.
That is where the priests came and fell on their face.

On this day, Peter entered the outer Jewish court
and he saw something that pulled him up short.
There was a lame man, a beggar so very bold,
who had daily lain there, now forty years old.

He sized up Peter and John with his keen eye
beginning to beg of them as they passed by.
Peter put his hand in his pocket, the beggar gleamed,
This would be much easier than it first seemed.

But Peter withdrew his hand, empty without coin.
He said to the beggar, "Silver and gold have I none."
But such as I have, I give to thee." Peter didn't balk.
"In the name of Jesus Christ, rise up and walk."

Peter's Undeniable Preaching

No longer is Peter denying the Lord or His teaching.
He is taking every opportunity to do his preaching.
He'd won many to the Lord on the day of Pentecost.
He is still trying to reach those who are yet lost.

Someone needed to go to Samaria in Gentile land.
But Peter hesitates, someone else they'll understand.
So, God sent young Philip to go and evangelize them.
Peter hears of his success and goes to check on him.

Peter told them he must preach what he'd heard.
This was another opportunity to share God's word.
Men of pride and of power could not intimidate.
He had to preach Jesus, and he could not wait.

Peter went to Samaria and took others with him.
He'd need witnesses of what happened to them.
The Gentiles were being saved as witnessed by others.
They were fast becoming to the Jews now brothers.

Peter had a definite distaste for anyone Gentile.
But the Lord spoke to Peter after a short while.
He sent him to the house of Cornelius and then
God showed Peter He was no respecter of men.

All of Peter's doubts were then swept aside.
God's love for the Gentiles could not be denied.
Peter's racial prejudice was very soon gone.
The church door for them was now open thrown.

Peter Returns to Jerusalem

The Jerusalem church had their case in hand.
Peter had done wrong and he must understand.
He told them Gentile salvation couldn't be denied.
They must be included; they had God on their side.

God had told them to go to the uttermost parts
and share His salvation unto all of their hearts.
These encouraging blessings widened his vision.
He must continue with the great commission.

Apostle Paul would soon be coming on the scene.
There'd be a different opinion coming up between.
But to Peter's credit he was convinced he was wrong.
And he agreed with brother Paul before very long.

After Paul took Peter aside for a piece of mind,
we see Peter change and thereafter we find
when Peter later wrote to churches, he'd recall,
he'd say remember, "Our beloved brother Paul."

Nero came to power and he made it his aim
to get rid of all who had taken Christ's name.
Peter knew his end time was now drawing near.
He'd escaped Herod but now his death is clear.

He would be crucified, hanging upside down.
We think of him as hero, a man of renown.
Tradition tells us this was Peter's last request.
His great spirit departed, going to its rest.

John the Beloved

We first need to see why John wrote this letter.
A lot has happened to the early church when he writes.
The first century of the Christian era is about to close.
John's now seeing many differences, and none delights.

The Jewish people have been uprooted and scattered.
The church is now spreading over the entire world, too.
John's endured the persecutions of Nero and Domitian.
The roots of apostasy have easily now come into view.

Christianity is now changed and hardly recognizable.
Peter has gone, James has gone, and Apostle Paul, too.
So, John writes to the third generation of Christians.
They are in desperate need of revival to renew.

In the 1st generation, truth was a conviction.
Those who hold a conviction, hold it ever fast.
They do not know the meaning of compromise.
They are willing to die for it, assuring it will last.

In the 2nd generation, conviction becomes a belief.
Sons hold to the truth that their fathers taught.
They will defend their beliefs with much discussion.
The keen edge of conviction has to be sought.

In this 3rd generation, belief has become an opinion.
Some members of the movement are willing to trade.
Taking up any promise that would be a fair exchange.
John writes with much urgency, trying to persuade.

John As a Person

John's father was Zebedee, a successful fisherman.
John's mother was Salome, who had many a plan.
She, herself, would often be found following Him.
She loved Jesus, His disciples and served all of them.

John was the brother of James, both heard the call
to follow after Jesus and they gave Him their all.
John was one of the inner-circle of the favorite three.
He wanted to be wherever Jesus Christ would be.

John the beloved was called to be one of the first two.
"The disciple whom Jesus loved," and counted on, too.
Jesus would later send him the Passover to prepare,
to make sure everything was ready for them there,

It was later that he was entrusted with the care
of Jesus' mother Mary, beneath the cross in despair.
John was contemplative, but he could boisterous be.
Jesus called him, "a son of thunder," so lovingly.

John was with Peter when the lame man was healed that day.
He appeared before the Sanhedrin, they wouldn't obey
saying the name 'Jesus' both were now to cease.
They admonished them both and gave them release.

John was banished to the isle of Patmos, we read,
living out the rest of his life having not much need.
Hastening his death was the Romans big plan.
What could the devil do with such a great man?

John As a Pupil

John's three and a half years with Jesus were well spent.
John's book is about what was said and where they went.
We have his memories that he wrote as an old man.
He has forgotten nothing he learned in his life span.

He's had ample time to think over all of Jesus' teaching.
And the things he tells us certainly are not far reaching.
Having a remarkable memory, quickened by the Holy Spirit.
He has much to relate, and he wants each of us to hear it.

John struck the dominate notes of the gospel in his book.
Wanting us to know Jesus as he invites us to take a look.
He wanted to demonstrate that Jesus was who He said.
He chose precise miracles, even Lazarus rising from the dead.

Seven times he referred to Scriptures being fulfilled.
He used the Old Testament often explaining as he willed.
He probably had Luke's gospel when he picked up his pen.
Whatever Luke had left out, John was sure to put in.

John taught us what he'd learned, easy for us to see.
John was the one who wrote of His absolute deity.
Jesus' upper room talks with His disciples at hand.
John reveals many secrets to help us understand.

John's gospel, mostly written about the "Passion Week"
tells us Jesus' thoughts, the many things He did speak.
The great wonder of the universe was Jesus' plan:
that the Son of God should die for sinful man.

John The Prisoner

In the Aegean Sea between Asia Minor and Greece,
John is sent by Domitian, with no hope of release.
Tradition says the Romans tried to boil him in oil.
He now is banished without any chance of recoil.

He is a much older man, still very much alive.
He is sent here to Patmos in the year A.D. 95.
We can picture him working in hard labor all day.
But he smiles knowing the truth, life, and the way.

Here he writes out his visions and dreams and, thus,
we know the future that surely awaits all of us.
He gives us visions of splendor in the Glory Land.
He writes the Revelation with his pen in hand.

The lone surviving apostle, by no means defeated.
He knows one day, by Jesus Christ he'll be seated.
He could not be eliminated by the power of hell
even though he's a prisoner, he's doing quite well.

What could the devil do with such a godly man?
Turning him loose was certainly not their plan.
He would only seek others, their souls to win.
Though they didn't believe in salvation from sin.

He is locked up in a penal colony but has words to say,
"Even so, come, Lord Jesus." He would go home to stay.
Jesus gives words of comfort, on which we can depend.
John has proven his faithfulness until the very end.

James

James was also a son of his father Zebedee.
He made his living working in and on the sea.
He was also a disciple, but we know not well
the things he did. The Bible does not really tell.

Most of the time, James is out of our sight
going about doing whatever he knew as right.
Most of time he is there with Peter and John.
But we do not often see him in what's going on.

When Jesus called John and James that day,
it seems their father put nothing in their way.
He had hoped that they would stay and help him.
Some even criticized him for going with them.

We're aware of the mother's scheme she employs.
She only wants what she thinks best for her boys.
She knows that Jesus did not have to persuade.
She reconciles to the decision her boys had made.

Of the two brothers, James seems to be the older.
John was closer to Jesus and was somewhat bolder.
Their love for Jesus helped them quickly realize
it was more enduring than any of their earthly ties.

James had some amazing stories that he could tell.
He was mostly content making sure all went well.
He was the cousin of Jesus. His mother took pride
that both James and John were at Jesus' side.

James Had Faith

James became a disciple after what he heard, what he saw.
He was there at the healing of Peter's mother-in-law.
He became part of the inner circle made up of the three.
He and his brother John and Peter were close as could be.

Jesus chose for James to be with Him at specific times.
At three significant occasions when his faith would climb:
When the daughter of Jairus the ruler was now dead,
James was there when Jesus raised her out of bed.

James looked upon the face, now cold and fixed in death,
He saw Jesus take her hand and she received her breath.
His faith was strengthened as he watched by the hour.
He saw Jesus as He conquered death in all of its power.

James was also with Jesus at Transfiguration's Mount.
He saw more wonderful things than he could ever count.
He saw the Lord's appearance change, what a sight to see.
He caught a glimpse of man as God intended him to be.

Jesus took the three with Him when He went to pray
there in the garden. The three went to sleep right away.
Jesus excused their willingness saying, "The flesh is weak."
James was with Him when the soldiers came to seek.

James was in the upper room when the Lord appeared.
He was so ashamed of himself because he had feared.
He made up his mind he'd never play the coward again.
He schooled his heart and went on, many souls to win.

Nathanael the Guileless

Nathanael was fortunate in the friends he had.
Philip was one of those, always making him glad.
As soon as the Lord Jesus found Philip that day.
Philip ran to find Nathanael to show him the way.

Philip was brimming over with the great news.
Nathanael sees him coming once he's into view.
"We have found Him, whom Moses in the law,
and prophets wrote about." Nathanael came and saw.

Nathanael, slumbering under a fig tree that day,
shook his head at the news and began then to say,
"Is there anything out of Nazareth that is good?"
The Jews tried not to think of Nazareth if they could.

Thus it was that when Philip added the words.
Nathanael might've argued at what he had heard.
He could have doubted this man from Galilee.
Philip simply said to Nathanael, "Come see!"

"Come and see," said Philip and it did not take long
for Nathanael to realize that he was very wrong.
He found himself talking to goodness that day.
He wanted to hear everything Jesus had to say.

He was confronted by a sincerity that soon made
all of his pretense and sham very quickly to fade.
With that arresting voice and eyes that could SEE.
Nathanael saw for himself where he needed to be.

Nathanael Meets Jesus

When Nathanael came to Jesus that day to meet
and see if his search has now been complete.
Jesus said, "Before Philip called unto thee,
I saw you sitting there under the fig tree."

That fig tree may not have been very tall,
but Nathanael went there to get away from all.
Maybe he was musing over Scripture's attention.
But Jesus was careful not to fail to mention

the fact we cannot hide from God is so true.
Jesus so simply told Nathanael, "I saw you."
Jesus described Nathanael as an Israelite indeed
"in whom is no guile." Jesus had a great need.

"Whence knowest Thou me?" he quickly inquired.
He had no 'tricks of the trade' that others desired.
If Nathanael said it, then it must be the truth.
He was direct that way even from his youth.

Nathanael, called Him "Rabbi." To him it was clear,
"Thou art God's Son, King of Israel, standing here."
Nathanael was far ahead of others in comprehension.
Calling Him King of Israel relieved all tension.

There are a few things in the Bible telling his story.
We know he was faithful all the way to glory.
What wonderful things did he do, did he see
in those years of his ministry after Calvary?

Simon the Zealot

We do not know much about this man.
He was chosen as one of Jesus' disciple band.
The other Simon is more easily seen.
"One who hears" is what his name doth mean.

Jesus knew Simon was a Zealot by name.
He chose him, He called him, and he came.
Jesus knew Simon had convictions in his heart
and he would be faithful right from the start.

In the band of disciples, he didn't seem to fit.
But he saw Jesus' authority had power to it.
Jesus cleansed the temple of merchants, indeed.
Simon the Zealot thought He was fulfilling the need.

Jesus had come to destroy sin's powerful empire.
Simon wanted to be part of what that did require.
Jesus had said, "Except a man be born again,
He cannot see the kingdom of God." Amen.

So, Simon the Zealot, for Christ made his decision.
He gave up his life of being a zealot in derision.
He accepted Christ's challenge, giving up his old life.
He is now one of the twelve, taking on their strife.

Simon's zeal would now need to be redirected.
There would be people by him soon effected.
Simon remained zealous to his life's the very end.
The church needs people who will be Jesus' friend.

Matthew

Mathew was minding his own business that day
when Jesus came by his table and took him away.
He had been collecting taxes a good while we see.
Jesus simply said to Matthew, "Levi, come follow me."

We do not know how Matthew became thus employed.
We suspect his parents were with him very annoyed.
It was unusual that a Jew would collect on their own.
Here sat 'Matthew, the tax collector' as he was known.

Jesus had a handful of new disciples close at hand.
He stopped before Matthew and gave His command,
"Follow Me." He said with no more explanation.
Matthew got up quickly without any hesitation.

Matthew had been yearning for just such a call.
He gives to his assistant his books, pencils, and all.
He didn't say, "I'll think on it." He got up and went.
He will now follow Jesus until his life is spent.

He was used to assessing values of any different kind.
But now following Jesus is the first on his mind.
He threw a party for his friends, inviting all of them.
He wanted his friends to come and to meet Him.

We have no idea how many came there to meet
the Man who changed Matthew's life so complete.
Matthew's gospel writings give to us the full text.
He had firsthand knowledge of what Jesus did next.

Matthew's Manuscript

Matthew wrote a gospel that bears his name.
He tells of the ancestry from where Jesus came.
He wanted the Jews to know of their great need.
The man they rejected was their Messiah indeed.

We have ample evidence of his specific intent.
In the gospel of Matthew, much time was spent.
He often refers in his gospel to "the holy place."
He helps us to believe and all doubt then erase.

Matthew's plan was to have order in the respect
his logical order would have a cumulative effect.
He kept the Sermon on the Mount intact, no doubt.
Whereas, in Luke the discourse is scattered it about.

Matthew records about 40 of the parables for us.
He examples the wheat and tares together, thus,
we see we grow together until the very end.
The judgment will come, the wheat will contend.

Seven of the parables say judgment is to come.
Not all will be ready, there will surely be some.
Matthew sticks to his purpose and will emphasize.
Israel's Messiah was standing before their very eyes.

Jesus warned that judgment would come upon them.
But they cared not and would not listen to Him.
The King is revealed and then resisted, rejected.
He is killed for our sin but in three days resurrected.

Matthew Reveals the King

The gospel of Matthew reveals to us God's Son:
who He was, where He went, things that were done.
He told us of the wise men who came from the east.
The Gentile magi who bore tribute on their beasts.

The King's purpose was revealed in the men He chose.
The King intended to administer His kingdom by those.
He bypassed the synagogue and the Sanhedrin and went
straight to common people as followers, filling His intent.

Matthew tells of His power, never before seen by man.
He cleansed the leper, stilled the storm by raising His hand,
He healed the sick, gave sight to the blind, raised the dead,
giving the dumb speech, and the multitude that was fed.

Yet the people resisted Him and what He wound bring.
They did not want to recognize Him as being their King.
They accused Him, saying it was through Satan He acted.
The good that He would do was severely impacted.

In the Olivet discourse, He told of destruction complete
of Jerusalem and the temple's falling down in defeat.
The events happened quickly after the warning of this.
Judas defected to the Sanhedrin, betrayed Him with a kiss.

Jesus was taken in the garden where he'd gone to pray.
They came in great force and soon took Him away.
They persecuted Him with no disciple to defend.
We read that this age has now come to an end.

Judas and His Crime

The life of Judas in the New Testament is scattered about.
We read what we can, but we are still left in doubt.
We try to piece it together but find it is all in vain.
We have more questions than answers that remain.

Did he have any brothers? Where did his life go sour?
Was it possible he was born for just such an hour?
Ringing out through the centuries, people hear his name.
It has since become a synonym for treachery and shame.

He stands forth as the very chiefest of them all.
His greatest acclaim is that of his betrayal downfall.
He is very well known, due to the tactics he employed.
He deceived, he despised, and he also destroyed.

There is no doubt at playacting he was a good hand.
He pretended to be devoted to Jesus' every command.
His credentials weren't questioned, he seemed okay.
He was treated as a brother from the very first day.

There's not the slightest hint of an exception in his case.
In the disciples much work, he had taken his place.
He held the 'office' of treasurer in this close few.
He took care of the finances and knew what to do.

One night they sat down together to break bread.
Jesus told them, "He would be deceived," He said.
Judas allowed himself to eat as he supped with them.
Not one of the brethren suspected that it was him.

People of the New Testament

Judas Despised it All

A lot of things we can learn about Judas' heart.
He actually despised Jesus, right from the start.
He called Jesus 'Rabbi' instead of using 'Lord.'
Refusing His name, His character, and His word.

It was a long time before that wickedness showed.
But it was there all along and it growed and growed.
Judas had the opportunity to grow ever close.
But he was not the disciple the others suppose.

He knew of all the miracles that Jesus did perform.
Some were done in private, which was the norm.
We can well believe that Judas was astounded,
not accepting the basis on which they were founded.

Jesus' enemies exclaimed, "Never a man like this man."
Yet Judas, all the time was making up his plan.
Hearing the words of Jesus was giving him pause.
How could he salvage something out of this cause?

The Lord could read his thoughts like an open book.
He deceived the disciples, but he couldn't Jesus' look.
"Have I not chosen the twelve," Jesus had asked.
"And one of you is a devil" doing the devil's task.

In the upper room Jesus said, "One of you will betray."
"Is it I?" Judas asked, to throw suspicion away.
In the garden soon after, Jesus called him "Friend."
Judas then kissed Him, the beginning of the end.

Judas Crossed the Line

Judas pushed back from the table and left the room.
We learn it was the next step in sealing his doom.
The others thought he had gone to the poor at least
or to make further provision for their continued feast.

"What thou doest, do quickly." He disappeared from sight.
And he went out, the Holy Spirit declares, "and it was night."
"Satan entered into him," the Holy Spirit doth relate.
Satan will soon take Jesus and no longer have to wait.

Judas may have thought, though his thinking is vain
that Jesus would but escape from His enemies again.
Judas was soon sorry for what he had done.
But did not seek repentance from the Holy One.

The money in his purse is now burning a hole.
He goes to the Sanhedrin to reverse his role.
The priests scoffed at him. "I have sinned," he said.
"What is that to us?" knowing Jesus would soon be dead.

He then flung those cursed coins onto the floor.
The priests scooped them up, they would buy more.
Judas went out and hanged himself from a tree
about the time Jesus was preparing for Calvary.

"He went to his own place," out into eternal night.
If he had gone to Calvary, he could have made it right.
At the Great White Throne, he'll come again into view.
"Depart from Me, ye cursed. I never knew you."

Jude

Jesus made His selection after a night of prayer.
We see Jude with the chosen gathered there.
He's barely mentioned outside the apostle's list.
Yet his little book in the New Testament does exist.

Jesus saw something in him, though he would not
stand out like Peter or John, he was one of the lot.
We do not read of great things he has also done.
But we do know he was faithful to God's only Son.

Jude asked a question, "Lord, how wilt Thou manifest
Thyself unto us, and not unto the world?" all the rest.
They had anticipated an earthly kingdom right away
that Jesus would set it up in the temple any day.

The Lord didn't deal with Jude's question right away.
The Holy Spirit would answer it for them one day.
They would grasp it more fully and take it in hand
when they were better equipped to then understand.

Jesus said, "If a man loves Me, he will keep My word."
That's the ultimate test of genuine love for the Lord.
Jude listened to Jesus' words and took them all in.
He said he would do all that his Lord did intend.

Jude tarried in Jerusalem along with all the rest.
He witnessed a great influx of souls and did his best.
This little-known foot soldier preached and did well
until in Persia, he suffered martyrdom, historians tell.

Andrew

Andrew was chosen, one of the Lord's first two.
He went and got Peter, "Come, let me show you."
He was always used to doing things Peter's way.
Here are the two brothers, together again today.

Andrew was not ashamed; he would say it out loud,
"Yes, I'm Peter's brother," because he was proud.
Peter got to see things Andrew did not get to see.
But Andrew was first chosen, that made him happy.

Andrew was a disciple of John the Baptist already.
He followed him closely and was ever so steady.
But the day John introduced Jesus to all of them.
He stopped following after John to go after Him.

For Andrew, this was a most personal quest.
Soon after he was followed by all of the rest.
"Come, spend the evening with Me," Jesus invited.
It must have been memorable, Andrew was excited.

Andrew and his friend John followed close behind
all of that day and into the night, they did not mind.
They'd be changed forever, never again be the same.
They knew who He was, and they accepted His name.

Andrew remained true to Jesus, hereafter we learn,
in the upper room he waited for Jesus' soon return.
Tradition says he was martyred doing the Lord's task.
Telling people about Jesus, whether or not they asked.

Andrew Was a Go Getter

When Andrew first learned that the Lord was near,
he went after brother Peter so he also could hear.
We find him bringing people to meet God's Son.
We can see his evangelism had already begun.

That was the beginning, him bringing his brother.
But soon after in scripture, he brings yet another.
People had been following Jesus, it now is late.
They are all hungry and they have not yet ate.

Jesus told His disciples to go ahead and feed,
but they had nothing to satisfy their great need.
Andrew surveyed the crowd, seeing what they had.
He found one had a lunch basket, such a small lad.

He took the young lad to Jesus right away.
They would see a great miracle performed today.
The young lad's mother had made sure that he
would have food to eat and not go hungry.

Jesus took the lad's basket that Andrew had found
and had the multitude of people sit on the ground.
Five loaves and two fishes were prepared inside.
Jesus took, blessed, and brake them to provide.

Andrew and the disciples fed that great crowd.
The young lad could never have been more proud.
It was Andrew's nature to bring people to Him.
Andrew always wanted to be a blessing to them.

Philip The Plodder

The name Philip is a much-used name, we see in fact
that he really does not have a huge impact.
His involvement in Jesus' ministry does exist.
He is listed as number five and the disciple's list.

Philip knew that Jesus had come to redeem,
armed with might and miracle, not as it would seem.
He knew the suffering Messiah who was now born
would one day from this world be violently torn.

Philip was not hasty to make up his mind.
He took his time, the real truth to find.
He had read all that Moses had to say.
The seeking sinner was found by Jesus that day.

Philip was trying to find Jesus in all that he read.
But Jesus was the One who found Philip instead.
He was pouring over old prophecies of sacred text
when Jesus found him, and we see what is next.

It is evening. The people had been following all day.
The disciples all said, "Send the people away."
Philip was asked, "Whence shall we buy bread?"
Jesus knew what Philip's answer would be instead.

"Two hundred pennyworth of bread is not enough."
Philip had taken a count, giving a number off his cuff.
"We don't have enough money, there's no way to feed."
Philip had forgotten that Jesus meets all our need.

Philip Falters

Jesus was in the temple teaching, just a few days ahead
knowing He was ending His ministry, soon to be dead.
In just three days, there would be the Passover event.
His life for the Nation of Israel soon would be spent.

Some Greeks came, they approached Philip to inquire
if he'd introduce them to Jesus while they were there.
They were proselytes of the Jewish religion but now
they were drawn to Jesus and His teaching somehow.

Judaism wasn't giving them the truth that they needed.
They wanted to meet Jesus, His truth would be heeded.
They thought with the name Philip, he would involve
himself with their problem and help them to solve.

Instead, he remembered when Jesus sent them out.
They were to avoid the Gentiles, leaving him in doubt.
He then passed them to Andrew to let him decide
if he thought Jesus would meet and take them aside.

Philip had failed to grasp the dispensational change
when the Jews rejected Jesus, things were rearranged.
Instead of his bringing these Gentile converts to Him,
it appears Philip gave the cold shoulder to them.

Later, in the upper room, Jesus said, "I go to prepare."
Philip asked, "How do we know God awaits us there?"
Jesus simply took Philip's comment in stride
saying, "I am in Him and He is here on the inside."

Elvis "Raz" Stephens

James the Less

James the less is what this James is called in here.
At least five times in the Bible his name will appear.
This man is known very little, giving us much doubt.
He doesn't ask questions, he did nothing to stand out.

James's distinction is that he was almost unknown.
He is very obscure, and he did things mostly alone.
In the church, James the Less always went about
doing things no one would do and carrying them out.

James was not a great apostle or prophet we find.
He brought people in who'd otherwise be left behind.
We all will go in and stand at the judgment seat.
James the Less is, for sure, one we all want to meet.

Before us will be the vast bulk of that city foursquare.
It is because of James the Less many will be there.
We see the jasper walls stretching wide on either side.
It has twelve foundations with strength to provide.

When the books will be opened, and we shall hear
all the wonderful things that he did while here.
Places he went, things he did, people he had won.
Bringing them to believe on God's begotten Son.

All of the unsung fellowship will take their stand.
Each of whom James the Less has had a hand.
One day, when we all get to that celestial city shore,
James the Less will be James the Less no more.

Thomas the Twin

We all know the name of Thomas (meaning twin).
In naming the twelve disciples, he's always therein.
The synoptic writers list him on their various lists.
We know little about him except that he exists.

We call him Doubting Thomas, which may be unfair.
He was overly cautious, wanting facts he could share.
He was the kind of man who wanted to be shown,
to be assured himself of all that was going on.

When Jesus said, "I must go to Jerusalem." It was he
who said, "Let us go with Him." Much danger there'll be
if Jesus was determined to go and there possibly die.
Thomas wanted to be with Him; his heart did comply.

Had they not gone, the greatest miracle missed.
Lazarus' raising from the dead tops the miracle list.
Thomas spoke from his heart, this time we find
but in his much doubt, he will speak from his mind.

In the upper room the 10 waited for Jesus to appear.
He told them to assemble, and He would come here.
When Jesus came to them, Thomas was not there,
they had slowly assembled due to their great scare.

Thomas, no doubt, heard He had assembled with them.
Next Sunday, Thomas was sure to be there to meet Him.
After touching Jesus' hands and feeling His side,
"My Lord and my God," Thomas then decried.

Philip the Deacon

The church in Jerusalem was overflowing with souls.
The disciples and prophets couldn't fill their rolls.
Jesus had told them to go to all places and preach.
But there were way too many here for them to reach.

The church chose deacons to help and to assist.
Philip was one man who stood out on this list.
The apostles were busy and in very high demand.
The Holy Spirit took Philip to reach another land.

So Philip went to Samaria and revival broke out.
Lives were transformed, miracles happened, no doubt.
The whole place was very soon turned upside down.
People came to Jesus from many miles around.

Peter and John came there to see what was going on.
Many were being saved, the new church they joined.
They preached in Samaritan villages, day after day.
But very soon the Holy Spirit called Philip away.

Philip responded quickly and quietly, going with Him.
He left the preaching to Samaria to each of them.
He met the Ethiopian's chariot in a cloud of dust.
And there led him to Jesus after gaining his trust.

The Ethiopian asked to be baptized right away.
Philip took him into the water there by the way.
Philip was transported away to do as before.
The eunuch, now saved, would see Philip no more.

James the Brother of Jesus

James was the brother of Jesus, it is known.
A piece of valuable information all its own.
He and Jesus had grown up, side by side,
yet James himself doesn't this info provide.

James was not like Jesus who went out to pray.
James was more into the traditions of that day.
James kept all of the forbidden things and, hence,
Jesus thought they had created a lot of nonsense.

When Jesus stood in the temple and spoke to all there,
James must have been embarrassed by the whole affair.
He wrote Jesus off as a fanatic and then turned away.
James could not see the forest for the trees that day.

James must have suffered when Jesus was arrested.
It was shame to the whole family, being thus tested.
He wouldn't go to the cross to be with his brother.
So, Jesus there assigned the care of Mary to another.

So then, what did convince James? We soon learn,
"He was seen of James." We see James soon turn.
The resurrection meant that Jesus was the way.
James is a pillar of the church since that very day.

Tradition tells us that he died so violently.
He was tossed off the temple's pinnacle, we see,
down where the fullers had their workshop of cloth.
Being yet alive, they with hammers did finish him off.

James Learns Then Teaches

James was a man like we never before saw.
He was noted for being a stickler of the law.
He became a presiding elder that exclusively
maintained that the church would legalistic be.

James did not know what to make of friend Paul
who brought in the Gentiles from one to all.
James was suspicious of Paul's different ways
bringing in uncircumcised Gentiles in those days.

James would later write a book in poetic vein.
He gives us word pictures that will remain.
It does not talk nor read like any other book.
He makes a moral appeal if we will but look.

He writes mostly of the works that we do.
About everyday things that come to me and you.
"Reading your Bible's like looking in a mirror with awe."
"Don't go away and forget what you just saw."

He writes about the tongue and what we say.
How it is uncontrollable, and often gets away.
We then will hurt others, saying the wrong thing.
The person who controls it, a blessing will bring.

"Submit to God," he says, "and the Devil will flee."
If I draw near to God, He will draw near to me.
Faith is important, but without works it is dead.
It is important we remember the things James said.

Nicodemus

We love the story of Nicodemus in the book of John.
He came to Jesus having heard He was God's Son.
He wanted to know if this heaven was a true deal.
And how could anyone go there if it was in fact real.

Nicodemus was "a man of the Pharisees," we read.
He was one of the religious rulers "of the Jews" indeed.
He prayed public prayers and taught scriptures to them.
So, we ask, why he is now coming secretly to Him?

This young Preacher that has taken Jerusalem by storm
was preaching and doing things out of the norm.
Nicodemus would meet with Him ever so privately
and show Him the error of His ways, clear as could be.

He came to Jesus by night so he would not to be seen.
He said to Jesus, "Rabbi." We know what that means.
"We know You couldn't do what You do," saying to Him,
"Unless God allows these miracles shown unto them."

He was about to learn Jesus was not an ordinary man.
That He was inhabited by God and had a heavenly plan.
And as God He was not just a teacher or a rabbi.
He spoke with authority as He told Nicodemus why.

In one sentence, Jesus would sweep everything away
that Nicodemus had depended on day after day.
Jesus knew Nicodemus was so utterly dead in his sin,
"You can't see God's kingdom except you're born again."

Nicodemus' Plight and Plea

Jesus had told Nicodemus that he must be born again.
You must be born of the water and the spirit to enter in.
The Lord not only revealed his plight, giving answer, too.
He said being born again is something that all must do.

Nicodemus asked, "How can a man be born when he is old?"
This startled Nicodemus; it wasn't what he'd been told.
He did not know what being "born of water" meant.
Nor baptism of the Holy Spirit was for those who repent.

"How?" Nicodemus asked again. "How can these things be?"
He'd studied the Bible since a boy, but this he did not see.
His Bible teachers had been the blind leading the blind.
He didn't know how to be born again, wanting now to find.

Thank God that he asked 'how' because most would ask "why."
Good behavior won't get you in no matter how hard you try.
Nicodemus wanted to go to heaven, so he asks Him now.
Nicodemus confessed to Jesus that he didn't know how.

The first thing we must do is "believe" — not just anything:
Believe on His name and the blessings that will bring.
"Thou shalt call His name JESUS" for He saves from sin.
Therefore, "Believe on His name," a must for you get in.

The next thing we do is "receive" the work already done.
I receive Him as my Savior, God's only begotten Son.
That's man's part: believe and receive, done in our heart.
He says we'll "become sons of God" and that is God's part.

Nicodemus And the Cross

Nicodemus stands up against the Christ-rejecting crowd
giving his own protest but not proclaiming overly loud.
They begin sneering at him and think he is out of touch.
He gives a favorable word, but he cannot do very much.

The significance of Calvary would soon dawn on his soul.
Jesus gave to the world complete and utter control.
Nicodemus then saw what the world was all about.
They wanted no part of Jesus and there was no doubt.

Soon after Jesus was crucified, he could more easily see
that the world was filled with values of great vanity.
The cross made a great difference in Nicodemus' life.
There's no evidence he was there, but he's filled with strife.

His cowardice and his compromise came flooding in.
He would never see, nor would he hear Jesus again.
Enough was enough; he could not stand this end.
He found Joseph of Arimathea, an old lifelong friend.

It was too late to undo the damage, but now he's bold.
We can picture this scene as it might now unfold.
He begged Jesus' body of Pilate that they might
bury Him in the new tomb and do His body right.

What happened at Calvary had opened his eyes.
It took away his fear and helped him realize.
If we are to come to Jesus, we must do what he did,
and make sure that our faith in Jesus never is hid.

Woman at the Well

There is a story in the Bible that we all love to tell
about the woman who at noontime came to the well.
She was likely the loneliest woman of them all then.
She was pretty and by far too popular with the men.

One can imagine the gossip that surrounded her name.
And why it was at noontime that to the well she came.
I think human nature has not changed one little bit.
Not even in these two thousand years it still doth fit.

The aged apostle introduces us to her on this page.
We do not know her name nor do we know her age.
Between Samaritans and Jews, little love was lost.
They avoided each other at whatever the cost.

The twelve disciples had met her as she came nigh.
They crossed over the road as they passed her by.
Bitter hostility existed between Samaritans and Jews.
Speaking to her was not something they'd choose.

So, they passed each other by and went on their way.
Wrapped in religious prejudice, making sure that they
had not demeaned themselves by speaking to her.
So, she continues to the well, her life is in a blur.

The sole reason she went to the well at high noon
would become an annoyance to her very soon.
There was someone already sitting there alone.
Of all the places He could sit. What was now going on?

The Woman at the Well's Life

He could sit somewhere else. Why was He sitting there?
She did not yet know who He was, nor did she give a care.
Yet He knew who she was and the way she did think.
He startled her by just asking her, "Give Me to drink."

"How is it that You being a Jew would ask this of me?"
She thought that she was as good as any Jew could be.
Now follows the wonderful conversation of these two
that John includes in this gospel for both me and you.

For her to have given Him water would've been a task.
She seemed to have no idea what it was He had asked.
It was difficult for her to draw the water she needed,
much less sharing the water in the manner He pleaded.

"Go call thy husband, and come hither," He did implore.
Jesus did not cover up her life's festering moral sore.
She had five husbands in the times that were past
but is not married to the man living with her last.

"You have no husband," Jesus said, "You tell it true,
The man you are living with is not married to you."
She quickly changes the subject trying a new ploy.
His identifying her sin wasn't something she did enjoy.

She suddenly felt ashamed of her sinful views.
Jesus did not say the word, He did not have to.
She knew she was stained by sin's awful hew.
Her story is a lesson for both me and for you.

The Woman's Witness

Such a conversation this woman had never had before.
Jesus told her what she needed wasn't just water anymore.
She needed living water that the Savior could provide.
He would save her very soul, and she would not be denied.

The conversation gets interrupted. Very soon we learn
when the twelve disciples came to the well on their return.
The woman left in a hurry, leaving there her water pot.
Her talk with Jesus was ended at its most crucial spot.

We see her silent witness as she leaves it on the ground.
The satisfying water for her soul had just now been found.
Maybe in her haste she is saying, "I minister now to You.
There are people back in town that I must go minister to."

The woman went into the city and sayeth to the men—
To five former husbands and the one she lived with then.
"Come, see a man, which told me all things I ever did.
Is not this the Christ?" They hurriedly came as she bid.

She brought the men to Jesus, and they believed Him, too.
What a change was made there as He gave them life anew.
Her new life was just too good to hold it in ever fast.
She shared the newness with those who knew of her past.

We should be the same way in our need to tell others.
We're all in His family, being now sisters and brothers.
We were also thirsting for the truth that will persuade.
As this woman at the well, what a change has been made.

Prodigal Son

The story of the prodigal son is a story of the father's care.
About how he showed his love that no one could compare.
It is a favorite parable for many of us who can identify.
We, too, are like this young boy and so often go awry.

The parables of Jesus are just miracle words He uses
helping us know the product of what each of us chooses.
This story, with the companion story, of the older brother
will help us understand how we are to treat one another.

The father did not run after the boy, as we so often find.
He remained, waiting long for him, always keeping in mind.
He did not search through the many dives and dens of sin.
He just let him go, praying God would bring him back again.

We know his father did certainly search for him every day.
He took his perch out on the porch staring down the way.
He thought one day he'll come home where he doth belong.
So, he watched and waited until he a righted his wrong.

One day as he sat and watched the horizon, with awe.
"When he was yet a great way off, his waiting father saw,
And had compassion and ran and fell on his neck, (we learn)
And kissed him." With great happiness he did now return.

"Bring forth the fatted calf," he told the servants to hurry.
"Kill it now and let us eat and let everyone be merry."
In the time he'd been astray, he had wasted very much.
How wonderful he felt now receiving his father's touch.

The Prodigal Son Thought He Was Having Fun

The Prodigal figured that if he left home and was gone,
he could have more fun, and he would be his own.
His father had rules that kept him well in line.
He would be his own man, and everything'd be fine.

The Prodigal decides, at last, that he has had enough.
Though he was well off, he thought he was tough.
He was tired of listening to what his father had to say.
So, he gathered up all his goods and went on his way.

This is always the Devil's first lie, "Be free," he'll tell.
"Please yourself, do your own thing; all will go well."
The Prodigal follows the Devil's lead, and he decides,
too many rules at home so his father's wealth he divides.

He wanted to live his life and have well-deserved fun.
So, he took all that he could and headed off on a run.
The path of sin is expensive, and he had money to spend.
In the far country, he found there many a new friend.

He soon realized it was 'fair-weather friends' he'd found.
As soon as he had spent it all, they were nowhere around.
Soon his resources are gone, and fun is no longer there.
But he had to sink even lower before he would care.

He went and joined himself to a citizen farmer there
who sent him into the field to feed his swine and care.
Working with swine as a Jew is not to be done, we're told.
At the end of the road in this world, it gets very cold.

The Prodigal and His Father's House

While the Prodigal's money lasted, he was having great fun.
When he is now penniless, he thinks of what he has done.
He had gone as far as he could go, as low as he could sink.
Now that he is in extreme need, he begins now to think.

"How many hired servants of my father have their bread
enough to spare and I perish with hunger now instead?"
The thoughts of home now begin to take first control
since the seeds of rebellion had taken root in his soul.

He begins to feel sorry for himself, after sinking so low,
he gives up feeding pigs and to his father he will go.
I will arise and go to my father and make this plea,
"I've sinned before heaven, and I've sinned before thee."

How he had gotten here was easy, it was all downhill.
But going home would be difficult, he knew that, but still
he knew his father was waiting and would fast receive.
His gracious father would forgive him, this he did believe.

His father has waited long for his returning one day.
He sees his boy coming home from very far away.
Despite all of the filth, the stench, and the disgrace.
His father holds him with the most loving embrace.

"My son who was once dead," saying to all around,
"Is now alive. He was once lost but now he is found."
Dead! Alive! Lost! Found! These four words tell us all.
They fit us when we answer 'yes' to the Father's call.

Pitching Peapods

My father was my best friend
on whom I knew I could rely.
And yet I was determined
to take all and say good-bye.
I had all I ever needed
but I wanted so much more.
So, I left my father's table,
closed behind me every door.

Chorus:

I left all the good things... that were for me in store.
Forgot all my teachings... what they had been taught for.
Put all my efforts into... my desire to make it big.
'Till one day I awakened.... pitching peapods to the pigs.

Then I started to remember
the many blessings of my past.
Got me up and cleaned me off
and headed home right fast.
To a loving father waiting
with meat and milk and fig.
God showed me something better
than pitching peapods to the pigs.

Do the chorus again: Then tag the last line slowly.

Prodigal Son Song (Number Two)

This song was written by my sister and she gave it to me.
I often sing it and I think it is a beautiful song.

In My Father's House (Bread Enough to Spare)

When I was lost and in despair... and nobody seemed to care.
I heard a voice saying, "Child, come unto me,
I'll set you free from all your sin... give you hope and peace within.
For in my Father's house...there's bread enough to spare."

Chorus:
He's my shelter from the storm... He's my refuge when I'm torn
and tossed about upon life's rough and troubled sea.
He gives me peace when I'm alone...
He gives me strength to carry on.
For in my Father's house... there's bread enough to spare.

I wasted all my earthly wealth.... sinful living ruined my health.
I was astray just like the prodigal son.
I would've eaten with the swine...
then I remembered just in time.
That in my Father's house... there's bread enough to spare.

Chorus:

So, listen friend... if you're not saved... and to Satan you're enslaved,
my Father's standing with His arms so open wide.
Trust in Him your every need... with His manna He will feed.
For in my Father's house... there's bread enough to spare.

Chorus:

Elvis "Raz" Stephens

The Elder Brother

When Jesus told the parable found in Luke fifteen,
He had a threefold audience to see what He did mean.
First there were the disciples who needed much teaching.
To them, this was a parable of faith and very far reaching.

Jesus also has the publicans and sinners in His mind
trusting that the kingdom of heaven they would find.
Finally, perhaps most of all, scribes and Pharisees at hand,
though they found parables much too hard to understand.

Jesus added an appendage to the parable of the son.
All of them did not agree with what the son had done.
The elder brother was a Pharisee and was very lost.
He did not want his brother back, not at any cost.

The brother kept the letter of the law, not in open sin.
But sin is sin and we can surmise, he held his within.
The elder brother stands as a biblical portrait who
holds their sin as better as those done by me and you.

They may not go to an excess, blatantly break the law,
they may not do any violence, none that we ever saw,
but they are self-righteous, often bad-tempered too,
putting way too much stock in all the things they do.

As we look at this elder brother, as the story doth unfold,
we find he is abstinent that his brother would be so bold
to ask his father's forgiveness, thinking all will be well.
We'll see here many truths this parable doth now tell.

The Elder Son's Displeasure

The elder son had been working in the field all day long.
As he approached the house, he heard merriment and song.
"What was going on that there should be so much glee,"
he asked one of the servants because he wanted to see.

The servant told him his long-lost brother had returned.
To the elder brother it was not good news he learned.
His father hath received him home both safe and sound.
We have killed the fatted calf to feast; we are now bound.

He thinks instead of this celebration that's held here today.
His brother should now be outcast and driven far away.
He thought, "It's foolish of my father, making all this fuss
just because the wasted wastrel has come home to us."

The elder brother entertains a thousand devils in his heart.
He welcomes all those demons because he wants no part.
He then soon became so angry that he would not go in.
"What? Go in there and welcome his brother home again?"

The father comes out to him but is very soon denied.
This brother is still angry and will not be satisfied.
"Lo, these many years have I not in all served thee
nor transgressed any commandment whatever it may be?"

If God were to take anyone to heaven for their good,
they would be cast out again just as Lucifer should.
Their pride would be inflated, and they'd boast no doubt,
This was the very attitude that kept this brother out.

The Elder Brother's Resentment

"Thou never gavest me a kid," he then to his father said,
"that I might make merry with my friends," as he shakes his head.
He resented what his younger brother had been able to do,
spend the father's resources then come home and begin anew.

"But as soon as this thy son was come," he begins to now state,
"which hath devoured thy living with harlots," with haste to relate.
"Thou hath killed for him the fatted calf." A gesture being made.
There is nothing that the father can now do to help to persuade.

But he tries. "Thy brother who was dead and is now alive again."
The elder brother was out of spirit, thinking only of his brother's sin.
The elder brother wants nothing to do with this fellowship today.
His mind and his spirit were unforgiving, a thousand miles away.

The father does not give up on him and makes one more plea.
"Son," he pleads, "as you know, thou art always with me."
He then gives a picture helping him to see, "All I have is thine."
The father loved the elder brother and wanted all to be fine.

They stood out in the edge of the field, being face to face.
He wanted this elder brother to respond now in grace.
We do not know how this great story doth now end.
The brother is left standing outside, his decision to defend.

We know Jesus will save all who ask 'cause He said He would.
But this brother seems to think that he is just too good.
So, he stands outside, unsaved— the father yet still pleads.
This tells us if we will go inside, He will meet all our needs.

Ten Men With Leprosy

As Jesus went His way, He met ten men one day
who had the dreaded leper's disease.
"Have mercy on us," was their cry. "Oh save us, lest we die."
In great love He healed all ten of these.

Yet only one of them returned once more to Him
to thank Him for his very soul.
He then heard Jesus say, "Arise and go thy way.
Today thy faith hath made thee whole."

Are we as one of these, who suffer from disease
letting sin in our life take control?
Do we from day to day, struggle on our way
as lost sheep, we stray from the fold?

Do we really care about what goes on out there?
Are we working hard to do His will?
Will he say, "Well done, a victor's crown you've won."
Or are we begging for His mercy still?

Let us thank Him for His Son, all that He has done,
changing our hearts to make us whole.
As did the one of them, let us return to Him,
thanking Him for the saving of our soul.

If but the one in ten can be saved from their sin,
is it not our duty to yet try
to spread God's Holy Word until the world has heard?
Let us try to reach them lest they die.

Ten Lepers

These ten men were "untouchables." Outcasts if you will.
Their haunt was the leper colony cave of the distant hill.
No one had lower esteem than these wretched wraiths.
Somehow, they'd heard that Jesus was coming up the path.

People fled before the lepers as they cried, "Unclean!"
Such a wretched sight like this was way too often seen.
These pariahs venture toward Him but He stood there still.
He would receive them gladly if that were their will.

He looked at their ravaged faces, as they looked His way.
"Go show yourselves to the priest," the duty of the day.
They knew exactly what His words to them did mean.
It was the duty of the priest to pronounce them clean.

In the Old Testament, only three lepers had been cured.
Moses, his sister, and a Gentile soldier had endured.
Some thought it was a hoax to offer them this purge.
It was a pledge and a promise to rid their dreaded scourge.

With eager anticipation and renewed hope, they went
hurrying off to the temple to see the priest, their intent.
And as they went their skin was cleared, it is revealed
that the leprosy remained no longer. They were healed.

As we consider these ten lepers, it is most easy to see
that they are unthankful, at times just like you and me.
We get what we ask for in the prayers we to Him make.
Then we forget that it was He who granted for our sake.

The Thoughtless Lepers

There were nine of these thoughtless ones
who did not thank Him for what He'd done.
We gather that each of them was a Jew.
They remind us all of both me and you.

In their mutual misery, they had tolerated
a Samaritan man not closely related.
They were glad he'd turned back to Him.
They did not want him to go with them.

You would think that all ten would return
but that is not the case as we soon learn.
This man came back alone so he could
thank Jesus for this healing so good.

Jesus asked him, "Were there not ten?
But where are the other nine then?"
What kept these thoughtless men today
from coming back to Jesus right away?

One thought, "I have family I must go see.
It's been a while now; they all need me."
Another thought, "I have great things in store.
Being healed now, I can do much more."

And so it goes, each has an excuse why
they did not return to Jesus to glorify.
Each one wanted to get back to their plan.
So, we return in relief to the tenth man.

The Thankful Leper

The decay and the death of the past has dropped away.
This is a new man that stands before Jesus here today.
He gives thanksgiving and praise for this life anew.
He wants to give Him honor for all that He did do.

The other nine, Jewish to the core, were then soon gone.
They were glad to be separated with this man alone
who stood there in giving thanks, this Samaritan.
He was healed; he was saved and became a new man.

Each of the other nine could offer a miserly excuse.
But this one stood above the rest ready to be of use.
He was going to enthrone Jesus today in his heart..
So back he came to proclaim that from the start

"Where are the nine?" He had many blessings in store.
They had their cleansing; He would have done much more.
They had no time to tender to Him their "Thank You."
He wanted to revitalize their lives, make them all anew.

We see it all the time, wherever the gospel's preached.
People respond to the invitation, having thus been reached.
They ask Jesus into their hearts right then and there
they are warmly received into the fellowship with care.

They are presented to the church, they are welcomed in.
But after this one meeting, you never see them again.
We do not want to be like the ungrateful nine of them.
Let us be like the leper who gave his thanks unto Him.

The Good Samaritan

The Good Samaritan is actually a parable about race.
It's told by Jesus, and it has three parts we must face.
"A certain man went down from Jerusalem to Jericho."
It is usually a downward path we all take as we go.

Men today convince themselves that we're on a rise.
This man left the safety of Jerusalem and did soon realize
there're those who'll rob and beat and leave you for dead.
The lawyer had tested Jesus, and this is what He said.

"By chance there came down a certain priest that way.
Seeing the man, he crossed over to the other side that day.
And likewise, a Levite, came to the place and had a look.
He too passed over to the other side, this poor man forsook."

Religion was no use at all to this robbed and ruined man.
The world is full of religions that follow different plans.
Jesus introduced them into the story so that all could see
that religion failed this man as simple as one, two, three.

The priest was going the same way, stopping only to pause.
He had fulfilled his duty in Jerusalem, done for the cause.
The temple of God and Jerusalem were now at his back.
He could not stop and address this poor man's lack.

His rites were useless in meeting the basic human need.
And so, he crossed over the path and did not intercede.
Thinking he had nothing to offer this half dead man, so he
went on his way and decided to just let the poor man be.

The Levite of The Good Samaritan Story

The Levite was of the same religious family as the priest.
He was of a different order. We'd think he'd help, at least.
The lawyer who stood up to challenge Jesus could see
and would recognize himself and the way he would be.

He had duties in the temple; he was a teacher of the law.
He would explain to people the rules of religion they saw.
He was to expound on the Ten Commandments given them.
And the 630 commandments they had given unto him.

He taught on compassion given to a neighbor in distress.
He taught that you were to help him out, nonetheless.
"If thou meet thine enemy's ox or ass going astray,
thou shalt surely bring it back to him again this day."

"If the ass of him that hateth thee, is burdened with a load,
thou shalt surely help him as he goes down the road."
The rules of religion, however, as embodied in the Levite,
does not mean that he will get this situation right.

He sees the poor man lying there, helpless as can be.
His rites of religion are of no help at all, we see.
What good would it do to tell him? He now needs aid.
Organized religion could do nothing if he stayed.

So, he crossed the path and traveled on his way.
Both the priest and the Levite passed by him that day.
They were traveling the downward path, just as he.
Neither of the two dared to help him with his misery.

The Person of the Good Samaritan

"But a certain Samaritan, as he journeyed by that way,
and when he saw him, had compassion on him that day."
The Samaritan was an outsider, disdained, and despised.
Though he himself, refused and rejected, quickly realized

being a half-Jew, he was the last man we would think
that would save this bleeding man from the brink.
We have no trouble identifying who this man doth represent.
It is Christ Himself, related in this story, as was His intent.

There had come a priest... likewise a Levite had passed by.
They neither one would help him, nor did they even try.
The Samaritan took up this man, showing great compassion.
Just like Jesus picks us up, we know that is His fashion.

The Samaritan bound up his wounds, poured some oil in,
put him upon his beast, and brought him to an inn.
He did something the others wouldn't do— he got involved.
To Him it was dangerous, but he got the problem solved.

First, he poured into the wounds, some oil and some wine.
That represents the Holy Spirit with redemption divine.
He did not leave him there as he found him but instead
brought health and healing to this man found half dead.

The Samaritan was on a journey and he could not stay,
"If there's any more that's owed, when I return, I will pay."
The Samaritan promised that he would one day return.
This is the sweetest story of mankind we will ever learn.

Elvis "Raz" Stephens

The Rich Young Ruler

I am going to include here a song I wrote about this rich young man
and then I will write a poem about him to be included also.
The song was written some time ago, but it says a lot about who we
are and how we think and if we are not careful,
we will become like this young man.

What Lack I Yet?

The young man came to Jesus seeking favor.
He called Him Lord, but He was not yet Savior.
He told the Lord of all his good behavior.
What lack I yet, dear Lord, what lack I yet?

The rich man came, his life was a disaster.
Not yet believing, yet he called Him 'Master.'
He wanted all and wanted it much faster.
What lack I yet, dear Lord, what lack I yet?

Jesus spoke the answer that was needed.
He went away, downhearted, so defeated.
And we can hear his lament oft repeated.
What lack I yet, dear Lord, what lack I yet?

Chorus:
I've worked so hard to build my worldly treasure.
I've gone above and beyond earthly measure.
I've given all to try to do Thy pleasure.
What lack I yet, dear Lord, what lack I yet?

Do the Chorus twice

The Likeable Young Rich Man

There are three rich men in the Bible, we are told.
Each of them is different, we'll see as we behold.
We see this rich young ruler as he comes into view
to ask Jesus a question, "What else is it I can do?"

Jesus saw the rich young man stepping fast with zeal,
"Jesus beholding him loved him," as he comes to appeal,
There's something about him that seemed to attract,
Jesus knew his need; he would ask what he yet lacked,

In excitement he cried out, "Good Master" he said,
Trying to say right things, he called Jesus 'Good' instead,
Jesus gave a challenge, "Why callest thou Me good?"
"God the Father is the only good." He quickly understood.

He then called Jesus 'Master' being ready to concede.
He wanted to ask about all that he yet did need.
Jesus gave this rich young man the greatest revelation.
The young man had not as of yet realized his situation.

"What is it that I lack?" he did sincerely ask outright.
He knew Jesus would tell him, shine on this some light.
Jesus reminds of five commandments dealing with man.
He says he's kept all of those the very best he can.

This young man was conscious that he needed more.
He was a ruler and had made hard decisions before.
He was very religious and was soon to openly say.
He wanted to find what he's looking for here today.

Rich Young Ruler's Sorrow

"One thing thou lackest," Jesus said. "Go thy way ,
sell all that thou hast, and give it to the poor today.
And thou shalt have treasure in heaven awaiting thee,
then come and take up thy cross and follow me."

Jesus offered an opportunity to therewith prove his love.
That he loved his neighbor and would now go above.
He had thought the Ten Commandments were enough.
Hearing he had to go beyond that would be very tough.

We can write two words across his life—'too much.'
He wanted to be a Christian until Jesus began to touch
his wealth and all the goods that he held in store
for he was one having great possessions and even more.

He wanted things to be on his own terms, we find.
So, he walked away and closed the door fast behind.
He walked away rejecting all that he had learned.
And the Bible doesn't give us that he ever returned.

His ruling passion was his goods, and his money, too.
He couldn't sacrifice, that wasn't something he could do.
So, we see him leave in sorrow, the shaking of his head.
He came with excitement, now leaves downcast instead.

"The love of money is the root of all evil." It is a sin.
Here in this story, we are reminded of it once again.
People put off their decision, waiting for tomorrow.
They too will walk away and great will be their sorrow.

The Rich Man and His Barns

In the Bible, we are not ever given this rich man's name.
But his appetites have a good hold on him just the same.
He had the kind of problem some folks have today, too.
He was so very rich he did not know what he would do.

The text records that he got his possessions on the square.
This rich man's land had brought forth grain to spare.
There is not a hint of any unscrupulous deal that he did.
His wealth was the result of God's blessings not hid.

He had prospered much, way beyond his fondest dreams.
His barns were full to overflowing, bursting at the seams.
He had no place to put the grain that in the field yet stood.
Where would he store this bounty with all of its good?

He says, "I'll pull down the barns and build greater still."
"Soul, thou hast much goods that will last you until
many years, take thine ease. Eat, drink and be merry.
"I am not an old man yet." So why should he worry?

Thinking to increase both his prosperity and pleasure,
he had an inventory of goods beyond all measure.
He left God and His Son completely out of his plan.
In the future he would be a well-known rich man.

"Thou fool!" The voice rang out like the knell of doom.
In the rich man's heart, he had left God no room.
"This night, thy soul shall be required of thee,
and whose shall all of these things then be?"

The Lost Rich Man

We have seen these three rich men and their cost:
The likeable one, lustful one, and this one that's lost.
This is not a parable as the two of which we've read.
This man was living once but now we see he's dead.

This is an incident, torn from life, history as we read it.
Telling this man's eternity, and ours if we don't heed it.
We are told that he "fared sumptuously every day."
He had been a man fond of ostentatious display.

His banqueting table had exotic delights to dine.
No less impressive his raiment, purple and linen fine.
But now he is dead and in a place that's very real.
He is in utter anguish and can remember and feel.

His pain was intense and endless and deserved
because he had not accepted, nor had he served.
This rich man awoke in Hades, now he would pray.
His prayer is typical and selfish as he begins to say,

He asked for a moment of relief, water, just a drop.
The pain he was suffering would not ever stop.
He then begged that Lazarus to his brothers be sent
that they would not come to this place of torment.

"If someone rose from the dead, surely they'd believe.
I want them to have a chance to new life receive."
This poor man waited too late, and he is now dead.
"Today is the day of salvation," just as Jesus said.

Lazarus

Lazarus is as rare a human being that can ever be found.
He knew what it was like to stand on resurrection ground.
He knew what it was like to leave this old world of sin.
He had glory with the Father, then was brought back again.

He could say, "Out of ivory palaces into a world of woe."
Only Jesus could say the things Lazarus does now know.
Lazarus must have decided that no one could be told
what was on the other side that would one day unfold.

Lazarus and his sisters lived in a modest home no doubt.
Jesus often came there when He was traveling about.
Mary was essentially a dreamer and Martha was a doer.
Mary didn't want Martha, the boss, to say a lot to her.

We can see the excitement when Jesus comes to town.
They know His favorite dish and ask Him to sit down.
Martha busied herself fixing Jesus something to eat.
Mary, as usual, again can be found sitting at His feet.

Lazarus come home one day, complaining of being ill.
Martha hurries him off to bed, bundling his body's chill.
Lazarus gets worse and his sisters think of Jesus then
"Lazarus is dying; we need Jesus to come here again."

Lazarus sinks lower each day, the doctor shakes his head.
In the bitterness of grief, Lazarus very soon is dead.
If Jesus had only come and healed when He could.
His death seemed much sadder than it ordinarily would.

Elvis "Raz" Stephens

Lazarus and His Savior

Lazarus was buried, and the days dragged on slowly by.
Jesus had not come and the sisters wondered why.
Then suddenly Mary and Martha heard the news.
Jesus is coming along the way to pay His loving dues.

Storm clouds were gathering in Jerusalem and Jesus said,
"Let us go into Judea again," going to Bethany instead.
Thomas said, "Let's all go so that we may together die."
They had no idea where He's going, and not knowing 'Why.'

Jesus knew Lazarus was dead, his soul we can be certain
was yet alive just beyond the other side of the curtain.
As Jesus came, Martha ran out to meet Him in the way.
Mary remained inside the house, she had nothing to say.

Jesus met Martha with truth, "Thy brother shall rise again."
She expressed, "I know he will at the resurrection then."
A truly great statement in the NT, Jesus to her doth give,
"I am the resurrection and the life, again now he will live."

Martha was comforted by the things in truth He did tell.
Then she sent for her sister Mary to come outside as well.
Mary came out with tears in her eyes and cried and cried,
"Lord, if Thou hadst been here, my brother had not died."

Then we read that "Jesus wept." Yet sadness wouldn't win.
He stood there amid sorrow, but He'd raise him up again.
He's indignant at the heartache Satan and sin brought about.
In Lazarus' resurrection, He will have His glory no doubt.

Lazarus Comes Forth

The next thing that Jesus said, "Take Me to the stone."
The multitude followed Him wanting to see what's going on.
"Take away the stone," He told those standing near.
Practical Martha objected with something He needs to hear.

"Lord, by this time he stinketh, being dead now four days."
All she could think of was the corruption the grave plays.
In her mind, she was convinced decomposition had set in.
And now it's entirely too late to bring Lazarus back again.

Jesus greatly overruled all objections, "Said I not unto thee,
that if thou wouldst believe, the glory of God you'll see?"
Jesus prayed to His Father because He wanted all to know
that He and the Father are one and He wanted now to show.

"Father, I thank Thee that Thou hast heard Me, and I know
Thou hearest Me always; it's because of the people that I do.
They stand by listening, watching all, and wanting to see
that they might hear and believe that Thou hast sent Me."

After praying, He gave the corpse a commandment to abide,
"Lazarus, come forth!" The soul of Lazarus came back inside.
The watchers at the grave saw him step forth tightly bound.
"Loose him and let him go." The bindings fell to the ground.

Jesus and His people drive a wedge that's very wide.
We are on one side or the other of the great divide.
We reject Him or enthrone Him, neutral we can't be.
Lining up for Him or against Him, now and for eternity.

Lazarus and His Service

The raising of Lazarus was only a week before Calvary.
He goes home to Martha and Mary, we're allowed to see.
We see Martha in the kitchen doing what she does best.
Mary is worshipping, staying near Jesus and the rest.

Mary comes to Jesus with some ointment, about a pound
and anointed His feet, the fragrance was soon all around.
She wiped His feet with her hair, Judas could stand no more.
He complained the money could've been spent on the poor.

Jesus said, "Let her alone, against My burial she has kept this."
Mary's worship was consummated, His death did yet exist.
People came from all over to see the new Lazarus there.
The man who was resurrected, whom none could compare.

The reaction to the witness of Lazarus is seen as twofold.
The chief priests wanted to kill him before this could take hold.
"By reason of him, many believed on Jesus," they decided.
This might be the way we trap Him; time is being provided.

We know what would've happened if this was done today.
Lazarus would be invited to talk shows to see what he would say.
But this is in the first century and Lazarus simply went home.
They had a simple meal together. In six days, Calvary will come.

Mary was worshipping, Martha was serving all of them.
Lazarus was witnessing to all who would listen to him.
This was a happy time for Jesus and His band of men.
Lazarus being raised from the dead, is now serving again.

Caiaphas

Caiaphas was the High Priest of Israel for about 18 years.
He was there when Pilate brought forth many fears.
Of the previous High Priest, Annas, he was son-in-law.
He was as wicked a man as anyone before ever saw.

He sinned against light, against law, and against the Lord.
He cared not about the coming of Christ nor His Word.
"This Man doeth many miracles," he grudgingly confessed.
He used the power of his office to keep Jesus suppressed.

It is hard to picture anyone being quite so cold blooded.
He appears to us over a dozen times as we have studied.
He organized the Jewish opposition, he was Christ's enemy.
He arranged Jesus' crucifixion, his name lives in infamy.

Caiaphas was insecure in his job, as we read. We can tell
the Romans put him there; they can remove him as well.
He knew that it was his father-in-law, as likely as not,
who, while behind the scenes, called most every shot.

From way down in Galilee, it came to him on the double
that a man named Jesus was causing lots of trouble.
He claimed to be the Messiah, and had gathered a vast
following of people who now clung to Him ever fast.

Romans had little tolerance of this trouble-making Jew.
Those following Him would be dealt with and severely, too.
As High Priest he had to deal with this, being in the know.
He was a growing threat to establishment; so, He must go.

Caiaphas' Corruption

With Lazarus being raised, everything changed for the Jews.
The entire surrounding countryside was ablaze with the news.
An emergency meeting was called by the Sanhedrin then
Caiaphas could not let anything like this happen again.

The members of the court expressed their frustration there.
"What do we do? He doeth many miracles with great care."
Instead of rejoicing that many miracles He had thus wrought.
They, as a group, decided that His life should now be sought.

Caiaphas said, "It is expedient that one man should die,
for the people, that the nation perish not," was his reply.
The Lord used Caiaphas' tongue to say this one truthful thing.
They thought Jesus' death would peace and quietness bring.

Then Judas showed up, playing into Caiaphas' crafty hand.
Although he had been with Jesus, he seems to understand.
He offers to betray the Messiah if they are willing to pay.
They offered thirty pieces of silver, the going price that day.

As Judas left with the money, Caiaphas had much glee,
"Now this supposed leader, will soon come to me."
Now it is only a matter of time, he thought with a grin.
We'll have Jesus in our control and we shall surely win.

In due time, Judas sent the word. Tonight is the night.
Caiaphas will send his armed escort, just to make it right.
No one could be too careful, Jesus could certainly resist.
Caiaphas had long been waiting for this capture to exist.

Caiaphas and The Trial

Things are working out nicely from Caiaphas' point of view.
They had taken Jesus into custody without very much ado.
One of the disciples had lopped off one of the soldiers' ears.
But Jesus had reattached it before he was brought to tears.

What mattered was that Jesus had agreed to quietly obey
and be taken by the soldiers who took Him quickly away.
First, taking Him to Annas; it's a courtesy call.
Annas bundled Him off to Caiaphas. It was his mess after all.

False witnesses were rounded up for some sort of trial.
Their testimony was so palpably false there'd be no relyal.
Other people were brought forth then to vilify and accuse
hoping they would give evidence that Caiaphas could use.

They kept Jesus there all night and openly questioned Him.
But He kept His silence and would give no answer to them.
Finally, Caiaphas asked, "Are You the Son of God this hour?"
"I AM." "You'll see Me sitting on the right hand of power."

Then, when the early dawn broke across the eastern sky,
they took Him so the rest of the Sanhedrin could ratify.
Then they took Him to Pilate who wanted to set Him free.
But Caiaphas and his crowd would just not let this be.

They'd carefully plotted how to get Pilate to understand.
They would use his fear of Caesar to force Pilate's hand.
This hated Prisoner would die, but not by stoning today.
Caiaphas had his victory, crucifixion was coming His way.

Caiaphas and His Cronies

It had finally dawned on Judas just what he had done.
He brought back the money to Caiaphas on the run
Those coins of treachery burned his pocket like a fire.
Taking them back to the temple is his greatest desire.

"I have sinned," he said, "I've betrayed innocent blood."
But this was far too late; it would not stem the flood.
He flung the coins at Caiaphas' feet, landing on the floor.
The priestly conspirators would buy the field next door.

The priests then hurried out, wanting to be at Calvary.
They would join in jeering Him; that was their priority.
They were very pleased with themselves, and they
cried out against Him as He was crucified that day.

But there were two members of the Sanhedrin who
broke away and went to Pilot and there asked him to
have possession of the body and to properly care
instead of just leaving the body of Jesus hanging there.

Nicodemus and Joseph of Arimathea stepped away
from the rest of the priests observed there that day.
They did not ask the permission of Caiaphas at all.
They would each provide for Jesus a necessary pall.

Joseph donated his new tomb and fine linen, too.
Nicodemus brought the spices, more than just a few.
Caiaphas made certain the Sanhedrin now had relief.
It was just another nail in the coffin of his unbelief.

Caiaphas and The Church

Caiaphas thought he had won but we see before long,
the church is now established and going very strong.
He thought the believers would disappear, having lost.
The disciples kept on meeting, then came Pentecost.

The church injected into history, a new entity is born.
The Holy Spirit has arrived, they no longer feel forlorn.
The disciples are all preaching, thousands being changed.
Salvation has come to them, Caiaphas is much deranged.

Peter and John were brought before him and he said,
"Stop preaching this Jesus or you too will end up dead."
They asked him a question, "Is it not better to obey?"
"Thrash them," he responded, "and send them away."

Caiaphas had a chance when Stephen was arrested.
He brought in false witnesses then to have him tested.
Stephen wouldn't relent, seeing Jesus by the throne.
Caiaphas had him condemned, dying by the stone.

When Caiaphas later reviewed the events, he found
a young man named Saul who would stand his ground.
He gave Saul letters to go search them out and bring
all of 'that way' back to him and he'd end this thing.

The church meant to Caiaphas an end of his evil ways.
The church is up and doing now forever and always.
They had wanted to kill the church, but we see instead,
Caiaphas and Saul had made sure the church was spread.

Pilate

As procurator of Judea, Pilate carried a lot of responsibility.
There were about seven million Jews he had to oversee.
If Pilate had let Jesus go free when they brought Him there,
it would've meant that he himself thought Him on the square.

Pilate rejected the claims of Christ to be outlandishly untrue.
Even though his wife opposed it, there's nothing he can do.
It was customary the governor would write the sentence out.
Who was being executed and what the reason was about.

"Jesus of Nazareth, The King Of The Jews," Pilate then wrote.
In three languages (Hebrew, Greek, and Latin) was this quote.
Pilate knew that Jesus was innocent of the charges brought.
It was jealousy of the Jews who caused His death be sought.

Pilate half believed Him, but he was yet a little afraid.
He knew Jesus was innocent of the charges that they made.
But he wanted to keep peace with the Sanhedrin, so
he washed his hands of the situation and just let it go.

So, to get even with the Jews for their annoyance that day,
Pilate chose the placard's wording, what he wanted it to say.
And He would not change it no matter what they pled.
"What I have written I have written," is what he then said.

The placard Pilate had written was nailed atop the cross.
They had begged him to change it, but it was their loss.
The title revealed Pilate's stand toward people he despised.
He disowned and denied the Christ which was soon realized.

Pilate Despised the Jewish People

As we read about Pilate, we can see he realized
that the Jewish people were people he despised.
He showed his contempt by the wording he wrote,
"Jesus of Nazareth the King of the Jews" is the quote.

Pilate probably chuckled writing Nazareth on the line.
It was a place to be derided, it was lowly by design.
Pilate's spies had told of this good Man o'er and o'er.
But Pilate had never met a Man like Jesus before.

Pilate had no trouble which one he would choose,
whether Caesar or the Christ, hated by the Jews.
When the time for the accusation that day came,
he wrote without any significance of the name.

Pilate asked, "What is truth?" of Jesus standing there.
Jesus had said, "I am the Truth," no one can compare.
But Pilate did not want to go against the Jews.
He signed the death warrant and this title he did use.

A crucified man would often linger on for many a day.
The Sanhedrin wanted Him dead, and they had a way.
So, Pilate sent his centurion their wishes to fulfill.
But He was dead by an act of His own sovereign will.

He had dismissed His own spirit and was at peace.
Death had overtaken Him but He would get release.
In three days, He'd rise again as He said all along.
Pilate's assessment of Jesus had been so very wrong.

Elvis "Raz" Stephens

Simon of Cyrene

There was a man who was coming through the gate.
The soldier drafted him, with no room for debate.
The margin suggests he was coming from the field.
"Pick up that cross!" he then could but only yield.

Jesus had made it this far but now all strength is gone.
He had labored under the weight but cannot go on.
He was trying to make His way to the hill of shame.
They drafted this man to assist, Simon was his name.

Simon had his mind on attending the Passover feast.
Just Who this Man was, he had not even the least.
But quickly he finds himself obeying the command.
He helps Jesus lift the cross, trying now to stand.

The centurion saw that Jesus struggled at the weight.
Jews were riled already, he chose this man at the gate.
Only criminals were crucified, or so Simon thought.
Such a shameful death was for those who were caught.

He'd heard stories of Jesus, things that He had done.
But he had never met Him. Could this be the One?
Step by step the unwilling Simon made his way.
He heard the crowd jeering, oh what an awful day.

At last, reaching the brow of that skull shaped hill.
With a sigh of relief, Simon disappeared, but still
I think he waited in the crowd to take into view
this same Christ crucified, dying for me and you.

Simon Is Touched

When Simon heard Jesus pray unto His Father, he knew.
When Jesus said, "Father, forgive them for what they do."
Only the Son of God could pray such a forgiving prayer.
Simon was touched that it had now come to this hour.

He had blended back into the angry Jewish crowd.
He looked on in astonishment as they cried aloud.
There were also two thieves, one on either side.
He heard them as they began to revile and deride.

Then one of them stopped, the cursing was now gone.
He begged to be remembered when He came into His own.
"Today shalt thou be with Me in paradise," Jesus replied.
Simon was amazed that the criminal was not denied.

Simon was troubled by what he saw and what it meant.
The rocks around the hillside were all torn and rent.
Word came that the veil in the temple had been torn.
A terrifying earthquake came, things looked so forlorn.

I think that day Simon was transformed in his heart.
He had closed his ears but I think he made a new start.
The Centurion had said, "Truly this is God's Son."
Simon could've also believed by seeing what was done.

People left Golgotha that day beating upon their breast.
"What they did was not right," many of them confessed.
This black man from Africa was used in their evil plan.
Surely Simon, too, went home a much different man.

Elvis "Raz" Stephens

The Centurion of The Crucifixion

We know very little about this man or his home.
He was an officer in the mighty army of Rome.
He served in the troubled province of Judea then
under Pontius Pilate. He was the leader of men.

He was a veteran of many a war we are sure.
He was a decent enough fellow having to endure
orders from Pilate that would put him at odds.
We see him leading Jesus to Calvary as He plods.

He only speaks once in all the events that day.
Out of the abundance of his heart, this he did say,
"Truly this is the Son of God." He confessed openly,
taking in what he heard and what he did see.

He'd received his orders of what must be done.
This had to all happen before the setting of sun.
He called for the cross to hasten and be brought.
The death verdict was in, death was now sought.

There'd been three trials, a death sentence in all.
The last one exhausting in Pilate's judgment hall.
Jesus lacked physical strength to bear up its weight.
They drafted Simon of Cyrene coming to the gate.

At last, they came to the place called Calvary.
Jesus' crucifixion would take place immediately.
The centurion saw that this was quickly done.
This long-awaited for event had now begun.

Barabbas

Barabbas was drawn dramatically onto the stage
of Christ's suffering and he soon filled the page.
He was in the background of Jesus' trial so gory.
Then he is suddenly dismissed from the gospel story.

There are a few words that sum up this man's life:
he was guilty of sedition and was full of strife.
His insurrection caused him to be a "rebel" they said.
Rome had caught him, he's a prisoner now instead.

His act of insurrection made him popular with Jews.
He robbed openly and violently, the methods he'd use.
He was as violent and evil a man as anyone ever saw.
A robber and a murderer under both Roman and Jewish law.

We do not know where he committed his lawless acts.
But we do know he was a criminal by the listed facts.
Matthew called him a 'notable prisoner,' not surprising.
He had so often fought against Rome in his uprising.

The Jews held him as a hero, his reputation undaunted.
Thinking him the kind of messiah they always wanted.
They always wanted a violent leader; this could be him.
So, they cried out that he then be released unto them.

He is what we would call a 'marked man' no doubt.
Rome had a price upon his head, wanting to take him out.
Barabbas had so many times justified his behavior.
How could they choose to free him and not the Savior?

Jesus Died For Barabbas

We see Barabbas sitting in prison with his head in his hands.
He had been captured by soldiers and must fall to their commands.
He had been caught and convicted and now must be condemned.
He finds himself now under lock and key in the town of Jerusalem.

The condemned cell is now his home as he mulls his many deeds.
The soldiers do not care for him nor answer his requested needs.
A verse or two may flash across his mind as he doth sit and wait.
His rebellion against authority will cause him to now relate.

He would look into his heart and see the mess it contained.
He would stoically accept his fate in the time that remained.
He'd stare gloomily at the prison wall and then he would swear
at the chains that held his wrists, keeping him anchored there.

He was doomed for crucifixion that would come just any day.
There was no getting out of it, his wrong he'd have to pay.
He had hoped to see the Passover, he wanted to do that.
But he could now hear the soldiers coming to where he's at.

He is seized by two soldiers who lead him out into the air,
into the open courtyard where the mob is gathered there.
They held Pilate to the custom, demanding Paschal clemency.
Hope blazes in his heart, Pilate must now set him free.

Pilate is going to use him as a giant gamble with the crowd.
"Which one do you choose?" Pilate was heard to cry aloud.
Pilate is now staking everything on a throw of the dice.
We soon see that Jesus died for Barabbas as 'his' sacrifice.

Barabbas Is Released

Barabbas thought that Jesus would surely be the choice.
As the two men stood there, Jesus did not use His voice.
One of the two by custom would today now be released.
He heard their mumbling, saw the busyness of the priests.

The scene was interrupted by a messenger of Pilate's wife.
Telling Pilate of her dream, "have no part in taking His life."
Barabbas had his eyes glued upon the governor's face.
Could it possibly be he'd be released from this place.

The priests would not waste the opportunity they had.
They worked the crowd into a frenzy, they became as m.ad
Pilate now challenges them again, "Wither of the twain?"
Asking, "Whom is it that I shall release unto you again?"

Chief priests moved the people, the answer quickly came.
The crowd cried out with each saying Barabbas' name.
"Then what shall I do with Jesus?" Pilate to them did cry.
The crowd in unison did cry out, "Crucify Him! Crucify!"

In a mocking gesture he presents Him, "Behold the Man."
The priests are now happy; this is according to their plan.
"He made Himself the Son of God," they began to cry.
"He is a blasphemer. By our law He deserves to die."

Barabbas saw the crowd's mood was going in his favor.
He didn't say a word, they would now crucify their Savior.
The eyes of Barabbas are now glued upon Pilate's face.
Jesus is his substitute and now will take his place.

Barabbas Did What?

What did Barabbas do? Did he walk out of the judgment hall?
Was he therewith celebrated and held in high esteem by all?
Did he then go home and become a law-abiding man?
Did he feel remorse that he was caught up in their plan?

Was he carried off by the crowd to begin to celebrate?
Did he quietly slip away to join those who for him wait?
The Bible does not tell us what it was that he then did.
It seems he must have gone away somewhere and hid.

We would like to think that he found his way to Calvary.
That he flung himself at Jesus' feet, now that he is free.
We'd like to think he asked Him, just as did the thief.
But there is no indication that he asked for any relief.

Did he then march with them up Golgotha's brow?
You can hear them as they sing. Did he join in now?
Did he also listen to their deriding and their jeering?
The Bible doesn't say he was there and also hearing.

Did he just walk away that day and ignore the Savior?
Did he erase this scene and forget their vile behavior?
Did he do what others do and just ignore the fact
that Jesus is the Lord of all? And he then failed to act.

The majority of the people today, as it was back then,
ignore Him as Savior, and that He'll soon come again.
We can accept the price that was paid for me and you.
Is that what Barabbas did? We wish that we all knew.

The Dying Thief and His Friend

On the day of the crucifixion, this was the scene—
a thief was hung on each side with Jesus in between.
At nine o'clock in the morning, you could hear them scream.
As they were nailed to their cross, they began to blaspheme.

The soldiers heave up the cross and drop it into the ground.
They laugh at their cries of pain as they stand around.
Above each head was written his crime and also his name
so that the thief's family would then share his shame.

Normally, people who were crucified did not quickly die.
Death would come agonizingly slow, days would pass by.
But the Passover was coming soon, the Jews had a plan.
They would have the soldiers break the legs of each man.

A soldier took a mallet and then snapped each leg.
It did not matter how much each thief began to beg.
One of the thieves had asked Jesus to remember him.
This brutal way of dying did not matter to any of them.

This thief died in one final flash of pain that day.
He had asked Jesus, who forgave him right away.
He accepted and believed the words that Jesus spoke.
And then in paradise that same day he then awoke.

He was not saved by confessing to the priests.
He was not saved by turning over new leaves.
He was saved by his faith in Jesus, so he asked.
So, I tell you friend, today that is also our task.

The Dying Thief

The nearer his death became, he thought more on his sin.
He hadn't cared for his life before the sentence he's now in.
Each pain-wracked, agonizing moment makes it worse.
He's encouraged by his fellow thief and begins to curse.

What better way could he vent this awful pain he's in
than to cast it upon Jesus, who is the Savior of all men.
Then he begins to think of what he has done instead.
"We receive the due reward for our deeds," he said.

He was suddenly haunted by the things he had done.
What they were doing was legal, but not to God's Son.
His cursing then fell silent, he realized he must pay.
"We are condemned justly," to the other he did say.

This was the prelude to his salvation, the necessary part.
There must always be a change taking place in the heart.
His conscience had awakened and now is fully awake.
He'll ask Jesus to save him for his very own soul's sake.

The very first work of the Holy Spirit in the human heart
is His convicting work which takes place at the start.
In a deep, quiet, mysterious way He will then come in
and will enthrone Himself in the conscience of all men.

The burning fire of death was licking at his feet.
He knew that his life would soon now be complete.
This condemned man was now dying as a thief.
But when he asked, Jesus offered him eternal relief.

The Dying Thief's Discernment

We do not know of anyone else who prayed for him.
But we are assured that Jesus prayed for both of them.
He had taunted Jesus, "If Thou art the Christ," he said,
"save Thyself and us," knowing they'd soon be dead.

He now looks at Jesus' face as He was hanging there.
The bruised and battered face, none could compare.
He lifts his gaze now higher, seeing the crown of thorns.
He thinks of the curse under which all men are born.

He lifts his eyes higher, the inscription there he saw.
He then looks at Jesus in wonderment and awe.
Not only did he look but he began to listen and to see.
The seven things that Christ spoke there at Calvary.

Jesus first expressed Himself in open tenderness.
Praying to God for their forgiveness none the less.
The thief flung himself into Jesus' spiritual arms that day.
This dying man learned his sins were all washed away.

The priests stood there at the cross enjoying this thing.
They'd paid out money for the satisfaction it'd bring.
They savored every minute. They began to rant and rave.
Yelling, "He saved others but Himself He cannot save."

So, like a flash of light, the truth on the thief did dawn.
Jesus was dying for the sins of man, not dying for His own.
"When Thou comest into Thy kingdom, Lord, remember me."
Jesus answered, "Today thou shalt be in paradise with me."

The Dying Thief is Delivered

Jesus looked at the man who had just appealed
knowing that salvation had now been revealed.
The dying man knew now who Jesus was and so
he asked to be with Him when Jesus did go.

Today! The thief would be with Jesus today.
Not many years later as some people would say.
Not after years in some imagined purgatory, thus,
Jesus receives the ones who die amongst us.

He would be with Christ in a very real paradise.
He had his faith and did not have to ask twice.
He was now saved and sure of what he heard.
This, from the cross, was Jesus' second word.

Soon after he was saved, the light went out.
There was darkness over all the land, no doubt.
The Savior had dismissed His Spirit with care.
The lifeless, shattered form was hanging there.

The Savior had gone on to paradise as He said.
He tarried for His new friend soon to be dead.
The soldiers came and put an end to his life.
But he was already forgiven for his strife.

A nail-scarred hand clasped a nail-scarred hand.
That day would be his first day in the new land.
He was then conducted into paradise no doubt.
Then all of heaven rang with a triumphant shout.

Ananias the Husband

Ananias is the husband and Sapphira is his mate.
The story in the Bible tells us how they relate.
These two names sound like music to our ears.
But their story is much deeper than it first appears.

People then were known for the grace of freely giving.
They wanted to be popular as anyone else then living.
They had a prime piece of property that they sold.
They would give the price to the church we are told.

Then it says that, "they kept back part of the price."
We know that deception is Satan's favorite device.
Now that they had money, they think differently.
"We don't have to give it all," they soon did agree.

There was an unseen Listener to their whispered pact.
The wife asked, "How much did you get for the tract?"
"Twice what I was asking for, he paid cash for the lot."
"Then let's only give to the church half of what we got."

"We'll tell everyone that we got such-and-such a price."
The Holy Spirit then warned Peter of their little device.
Ananias then came forth, laid the offering at Peter's feet.
Peter asked, "Is this all, now that the deal's complete?"

The lie that Ananias told made the situation worse.
He soon suffered for this sin and received death's curse.
Judgment fell on him that day. He now lay there dead.
"You have not only lied to men," is what Peter said.

Sapphira The Wife

At the church's meeting place, Sapphira now comes in.
We can imagine she is all smiles as she looks at the men.
By now their generous gift is what all is talking about.
She smiles and nods at each one, leaving no one out.

Too eager to receive the acceptance on each face,
she does not give notice to the silence in the place.
Then casually Peter asked her, "Sapphira, by the way,
the man buying your property, how much did he pay?"

She didn't see Ananias; he'd been three hours gone.
She wanted to protect him, but she is now all alone.
She answered with the lie that they both had told.
She was quickly worried, but she wanted to be bold.

"To tempt the Holy Spirit, both of you did agree,
and now it is that you must pay the same penalty."
"The feet of them that carried thy husband before
now shall carry you out, they're even at the door."

She had no time for reflection, the die had been cast.
She dropped dead at Peter's feet; it happened that fast.
"Great fear came upon all the church," we read.
The Holy Spirit showed His power and did intercede.

Almost anyone can join a church today as we know.
They have all kinds of promotions just to help them grow.
We close our eyes to discipline and promises they give.
It no longer seems to matter how they tend to live.

Stephen

The deacons of the early church were excellent men.
Stephen was of high prominence among them then.
We call him the first martyr for the church's cause.
Nero wanted to kill them all and he made the laws.

He would often stand them in his garden set afire
and would burn them as torches, his evil desire.
Satan would have them all dead, so he consented.
His attack on the early church continued unrelented.

The church was very giving and squabbles often came.
Each one wanted to be given the exact very same.
This problem took the apostles away from their work.
Settling differences, making sure that none were shirked.

Deacons were decided to be the answer they sought.
They made a list of men who could not be bought.
Stephen came immediately to the top of their list.
It is thought today, because of him, deacons do exist.

The law and the prophets' words, Stephen did fulfill.
Stephen developed boldness and followed God's will.
He would stand for hours, and he would debate
anyone who spoke of Jesus as being second rate.

Stephen taught the Scriptures with much authority.
He believed the resurrection was as clear as could be.
He taught that Jesus was the Son of God, in trust.
He died to bring us to God, the just and the unjust.

Stephen Is Stoned

Before long the Jewish leaders had Stephen arrested.
His faith and belief in Jesus was soon to be tested.
Stephen would give the best testimony ever heard.
As he reminded them of the scriptures' very word.

Stephen's defense of the gospel ranks at the very top.
His accusers were the ones who needed now to stop.
He reminded them of all the opportunities they had.
The elite religious leaders of the nation then got mad.

They had accused him of violating the holy place.
He would quickly answer them speaking face to face.
"Now hearing these things, they were cut to the heart."
And they gnashed on him with their teeth from the start.

He hammered home God's truth, then he looked away.
He looked up into Heaven and saw Jesus that day.
He instantly bore witness as to whom it was he saw.
It was Jesus standing, waiting to receive him in awe.

At least 16 times we see Him at the Father's right hand.
Thirteen times He's seated, but this time He doth stand
to receive faithful Stephen, who is coming home today.
They had tried him and stoned him; his soul is on its way.

Stephen prayed for the forgiveness for those men
who stoned him to death and was guilty of this awful sin.
His faith and his expectancy in God he did keep.
It says, "And when he had said this, he fell asleep."

Cornelius

The Jews detested Gentiles and couldn't stand them at all.
That is what is so different about Peter getting the call.
Just entering a Gentile home would render the Jew unclean.
For a Jew to assist a Gentile was something never seen.

The Jews asserted that God, of all nations, loved only them.
They could not believe that He would call Gentiles to Him.
In visiting the Jewish temple, they could only go so far in.
The Jews called it the 'Court of the Gentiles' back then.

If a Gentile came too close, he was stopped by a wall.
This 'middle wall of partition' was four to five feet tall.
On this wall, 'do not pass' was written as his command.
Written in both Greek and Latin so he would understand.

It had been eight long years since Pentecost and yet
the gospel was in Jerusalem; that was as far as it did get.
No one had gone to Caesarea to share the gospel there.
That's where the Gentiles lived, and no one gave a care.

God sent an angel to Cornelius in answer to his prayer.
"Send for a man called Simon Peter staying with Simon there.
Have him come and tell you of the much better way."
That's exactly what Cornelius did, reacting that same day.

Little did Peter understand what he was doing that day
going to Cornelius' home to hear what he had to say.
Peter put away his prejudice and put away his pride.
He went to the home where Cornelius' family did abide.

Cornelius' Invitation

Apostle Peter was staying at the home of Simon the tanner.
They had gone up on the flat roof and had their dinner.
Peter stretched out and soon fell fast asleep lying there.
His host left him to his dreams showing him great care.

He dreamed there were pictures of animals on a sheet
and a voice he heard saying, "Rise, Peter, kill and eat."
The animals shown were animals that Jews couldn't eat.
God was showing him all different kinds of clean meat.

Three times to Peter, this vision of the sheet occurred.
He rubbed his eyes wondering what he'd seen and heard.
The Spirit said, "Three men seek thee, you are not to doubt.
Go with them and you will see what this is all about."

We can hear his host Simon calling up the stairs to him.
"Three men are here to see you; a soldier has sent them."
The men had a message and an invitation to give:
You are to come with us to where Cornelius doth live.

It was down in the evening and Caesarea was far away
so the men spent the night and headed back next day.
Peter asked many questions; we can be sure that he did.
Christ to these Caesarean soldiers was not to be hid.

Arising early, the next morning, a group was on its way.
The three men and Peter and some witnesses that day.
They wanted to know what caused Peter to be sent.
They became impartial witnesses to this historic event.

Cornelius Has Revival

The centurion treated Peter as if he's more than a man.
An angel had addressed him as part of the overall plan.
The house was already packed when Peter arrived there.
People knew Cornelius would have an answer to his prayer.

Peter had an eager and receptive audience that day.
He began by explaining why he had come this way.
Why he'd accepted the invitation to the home of a Gentile.
Then he went straight to Jesus in just a little while.

Peter opened up the gospel and he began to preach.
They eagerly did listen, more and more they did beseech.
First, he spoke about Jesus giving His life in service, then
he told of Jesus giving His life in sacrifice for all men.

"Whom they (ALL ALIKE) slew and hanged upon a tree.
Whom God raised up the third day and showed Him openly."
Revival broke out in that home. There God saved the lost.
The Holy Spirit came down, just as He did at Pentecost.

This Holy Spirit's work was never heard of or seen before.
That unto the Gentiles would be such an effectual door.
Many Gentiles were saved at Cornelius' home that day
when Peter told them there was a much better way.

Peter and his friends stayed there for a good while
before going to Jerusalem. He knew there'd be denial.
It was difficult for them to accept the Gentiles in.
We find that in God's church, He accepts all men.

Cornelius And The Caesarean Church

Peter stayed and continued preaching to them God's word.
The Jewish church back in Jerusalem very soon had heard.
It is amazing how fast they heard as the word got out.
They talked bad about Peter and his preaching no doubt.

How could he even go into a Gentile home at all?
How could he tell them that God gave them a call?
That the Holy Spirit of God they could then receive.
Even with his many witnesses, they would not believe.

It was bad enough he went there, but he had remained.
He told the Gentiles, church membership could be obtained.
The rumors were embellished by the time he returned.
They could've excommunicated him by what they'd learned.

This is such a short time after experiencing Pentecost.
It seems the church's spiritual state had so soon been lost.
How could they put their chief apostle now on trial?
Because he preached to Gentiles and practiced non-denial.

Peter had failed to dot his I's like they wanted him to.
But he had done only what an apostle was to do.
He told them how the Holy Ghost fell upon them there.
He spoke only the gospel that God wanted him to share.

They didn't invite Cornelius to come to Jerusalem to meet.
But God already had a plan to make it all complete.
He had placed Philip there to carry on and he preached.
Today we're very happy that the Gentiles were reached.

Barnabas

The Holy Spirit tells us that Barnabas was a good man.
Due to his character, he fits perfectly into God's plan.
Barnabas was the kind of man for whom you would die.
He was a lovable, humble man, this we can't deny.

We first meet Barnabas at the church in its early days.
He was ablaze for the cause of Christ in all his ways.
He too shared all he had, his name was of renown.
But very soon the church's fire began to die down.

Barnabas was a Levite, his estates covered lots of land.
He sold it all and gave the money to the Apostle band.
Of all who gave possessions, no one could compare.
This landless man dedicated himself to church welfare.

He was a wealthy man and of nothing he did need.
He became a Christian Levite, a true Levite indeed.
He was a sincere man, his generosity gave him fame.
His service to God's family earned for him a new name.

His old man was Joseph, but that name changed quickly
to Barnabas, 'son of consolation and son of prophecy.'
When they spoke this name, they thought of right then
how he identified with Jesus because he loved all men.

By this new name he was from then on identified.
It was well known that he on the Holy Spirit relied.
So, this is the introduction to this well-known man.
He was well gifted to communicate to them God's plan.

Barnabas Is a Sympathetic Man

It was Barnabas who introduced Saul of Tarsus to them.
Three years since his conversion and no one had seen him.
The church had heard rumors that he was now a believer.
But they would not believe it; to them he was a deceiver.

He has gone away; they all drew that same conclusion.
God's saints enjoyed the blessed rest from persecution.
But now Saul is back, worse still he's come back there.
He's seeking fellowship in the church, showing care.

Everyone was frightened of him joining the church indeed.
To the most dangerous man of the age, they wouldn't heed.
The blood of so many Christians was still red on his hands.
The fact he was friendless was very easy to understand.

Barnabas alone, of all the disciples, opened up his door.
Things were much different now than they were before.
Yet Barnabas took him in and listened to his story.
How he now loved Jesus and to God gave the glory.

We can picture taking him to Peter's place and saying,
"I want you to meet Brother Saul, he will be staying."
Peter was so convinced that he willingly took him in.
What an eventful two weeks that must have been.

Barnabas was not the least bit jealous of these two.
He was such a sympathetic man in all that he did do.
In the church, Saul would become its pillar and its crutch.
Of Brother Saul, Apostle Peter would now make so much.

Barnabas Is A Spiritual Man

Barnabas has now gone to Antioch, there to assist.
After Rome and Alexandria, Antioch is third on the list.
Antioch is wealthy and of magnificence so sublime.
It was the third greatest city in the world at that time.

It was a Greek city with the grove of Daphne back then.
The home of the Roman prefect, his court, and his men.
It had a large Jewish colony, yet idolatry was its norm.
Heathenism flaunted itself in many an alluring form.

The Holy Spirit led Barnabas to come here and begin
a new work that would bring many lost souls in.
Here in voluptuous, sinful Antioch the gospel spread.
Soon people were coming to the new church instead.

It neither sought nor needed apostle support to go.
It took root on its own and began swiftly to grow.
Word soon got back to Jerusalem; and they inquired.
Some apostles came for the answers they desired.

Barnabas was indeed a spiritual man, as we read,
"A good man full of the Holy Ghost." He was indeed.
He was careful not to lecture new believers and so,
he led by example in the way they were to go.

"He exhorted them all, that with purpose of heart,
they would cleave unto the Lord," making a new start.
"And much people was added to the Lord," it is said.
He preached Christ, and the revival fires spread.

Barnabas Was Surrendered

In the Antioch church, there soon came a special call.
The Holy Spirit said, "Separate me Barnabas and Saul."
He called, no less, two of the church's very best men
to be missionaries to a world of folk who were lost in sin.

Of the ablest preachers and personal workers, these two,
chosen to go and preach Christ to those who never knew.
It was a missionary call of God to go to the regions beyond
to reach out to others of whom God is so very fond.

To go now to "the uttermost part of the world," he said.
Not just to remain in Jerusalem and Antioch instead.
To take the glad tidings to millions of people yet untold,
Barnabas and Saul had been chosen and they were bold.

Barnabas could have made excuses of the reason why
he could have said, "No, I can't go" and began to deny.
"I want to stay here; I'm more fitted to work of this kind."
But instead, he readily stepped forth in agreement we find.

Barnabas was surrendered and was very much prepared
for the work of the Spirit that he and Saul now shared.
The Holy Spirit was burdening the elders of the lost.
Barnabas and Saul were now ready to go at any cost.

Barnabas' goodness gave him the compassion he needed.
The call to 'go' was very quickly with competence heeded.
He had the compulsion and the willingness to dare.
Trusting God for provision, he surrendered to go and share.

Barnabas Is A Sound Man

The Jerusalem church wanted to know what was going on
down in Antioch. A great work was there now being done.
So, they chose Barnabas to go there because he was sound.
He would come back and report what it was there he found.

What sounder man could they have found than was he.
There was a need to send someone there just to see.
False teaching was being allowed by the church there.
They needed a man to go, one that would show care.

They wanted to learn what was the Antioch church's intent.
So, Barnabas and Paul (along with some others) were sent.
The issues at stake were enormous, false teachers asserted
that circumcision must happen or you would be diverted.

That made sense to the legalists; twas the natural outcome
of his Judaism, so they easily persuaded quite a large sum
who had come to Christ by circumcision and by the law
and by hundreds of rituals that no one else ever saw.

How could the Gentiles be saved, starting halfway?
False teachers said they must do things their way.
The difference would need to be decided and fast.
Having so much dispute wouldn't be allowed to last.

Had it not been for Barnabas, what would they do?
The church would certainly have been broken in two.
A sound man was needed to mediate this task.
Could anyone be more conciliatory than Barnabas, I ask?

Barnabas Is a Separated Man

The conference settles the division, and it is now done.
There will not be two churches, there will be only one.
To be a Christian, the Gentile need not become a Jew.
The good news came back to Antioch, they began anew.

Peter soon came there to take his own look to see.
Then certain legalistic Jewish brothers came in disunity.
Peter showed them favoritism, now sitting on the fence.
Paul gave Peter a dressing down, there was no defense.

Barnabas seemed to be more than willing to let it be.
Not speaking out against it he then conceded quietly.
Paul asked Barnabas about taking a second journey then,
but Barnabas wanted to take young John Mark again.

The Holy Spirit draws attention to their decision made.
Barnabas wanted Mark, but Apostle Paul was afraid.
This was not a small disagreement of dire suspense.
People took sides back then and they have ever since.

Barnabas wanted his nephew Mark, so he took a pause.
Young Mark was at least enthusiastic for the cause.
He'd turned back before, and he was thoroughly ashamed.
After all, he was kin, and he wanted him to be named.

Apostle Paul had forgiven Mark a long, long time ago.
But this trip was not for him and Paul told them so.
Barnabas parted then with Paul and went another way.
The Holy Spirit marched on with Apostle Paul that day.

Saul of Tarsus

Saul of Tarsus was a young man who was there
when Stephen was stoned after the testimony he did share.
He saw the blood that came forth that very day.
It turned him into a tiger and we can hear him say.

"Here fellows, put your coats and I will watch them."
He was totally in agreement of their stoning him.
They took off their coats and placed them at his feet.
This imperious young man watched the stoning complete.

Stephen will receive a martyr's crown at judgment's seat
and maybe a soul-winners crown that will be replete.
Saul of Tarsus would debate the gospel with all his kin.
What an interesting debate that must have been.

Never could Saul forget Stephen's testimony that day.
Friendless and forsaken but he stood there anyway.
Surrounded by bitter and hostile men, yet he was bold.
He said the things that of the Holy Spirit he was told.

Stephen looked like an angel as Saul watched him die.
Neither of the two men needed to ask themselves why.
Saul had not known anyone who would die as he did.
The glory that shown on his face could never be hid.

That angel face haunted Saul, and it troubled his mind.
He would remember this man because he was so kind.
Stephen became so much like the Lord at that place.
It showed in his countenance and especially on his face.

Saul's Conversion

The conversion of Saul of Tarsus was a miracle of grace.
It was the talk in every quarter and canton every place.
No one could believe that Saul was a converted man.
He was known for his rebellion, following his own plan.

"It would take a special dispensation," people often said.
"I don't believe he'll be converted. I'll pray for him instead."
But he did become a Christian in spite of all he'd done.
Of his mistreatment of Christians, putting them on the run.

Some are pliable and easily molded, but this is not Saul.
His personality was hewn out of rock, he would give his all.
He was enunciated by his teacher and mentor Gamaliel.
"Leave them alone if they are of God," is how he did feel.

But Saul did not agree, he said, "With Christianity coexist."
"Not me by any means!" and he asked the priests for a list.
He wanted all of 'the way' to be in prison or be dead.
He used his forceful personality for the fight ahead.

All his mind, soul, heart, and strength were soon set ablaze.
He'd persecute those of 'the way' the rest of their days,
He used the drive of his fervor and his eloquence until
all the Christians feared the drive of his unbridled will.

He became a mighty vehicle of destruction back then.
He was well known and feared by all the other men.
His hatred for Jesus and the detested cult of Nazarene
made him the most horrible man they had ever seen.

Saul's Violence of Persuasion

Saul had his conviction about what Christ ought to be.
The meek and lowly Jesus of Nazareth certainly was not He.
Jesus was nothing but a weak impostor in Saul's book.
Saul would influence others if they'd only stop and look.

He envisioned a militant Messiah, son of David, man of war.
The Messiah would smite the power of Rome like none before.
He would make Jerusalem the new world capital for sure
founded on the Mosaic Law and the prophets to endure.

Saul was looking for a martial Messiah, not one who's meek.
A 'meek Messiah' was a contradiction of terms he didn't seek.
He wanted a Messiah who let Himself be crowned as King.
A Messiah who'd let Himself be crucified was not his thing.

Saul wanted a Messiah who would set Himself up to reign.
Not a Messiah who would redeem, forgiving of all men.
The thought of Calvary was revolting, and he made it clear.
That scene shouldn't be the grand finale of His journey here.

The idea that great David's greater Son should die this way
being crucified by Romans was preposterous, he would say.
Saul knew his Bible. He knew the Scripture that said,
"Cursed is every man that hangeth on a tree" until dead.

That God's Son should hang on a tree, was outrageous to him.
It was blasphemy; He disliked anyone preaching that to them.
With Saul of Tarsus, there was no discussion and debate.
It was a matter of life or death that he wanted to relate.

Saul's Vindictive Passion

Saul nursed a fierce hatred in his soul, having the result
that he would go and stamp out this Christianity cult.
The Sanhedrin was only too glad, they hated them, too.
They gave Saul permission to do what he wanted to do.

They gave him a mandate; they gave him a free hand
to get rid of all the Christians out of all of the land.
Their dislike was confirmed by this young man Saul.
He would do their dirty work and get rid of them all.

In later years he would say he'd been "exceedingly mad."
He made 'havoc of the church,' the strongest word he had.
Greek scholars tell us that is the strong metaphor he used.
He went after churches making sure they were abused.

Saul had one controlling passion by night and by day:
he persecuted fathers and mothers, all those of 'the way.'
He wanted to beat, brand, and bully; he ranted and raved.
And he was in such a mood the very day he was saved.

He was on his way to Damascus in the blazing sun.
His attendants thought that he was almost on the run.
He was in a fever of rage wanting to get after them
before someone could get there and warn them of him.

So, the salvation of Saul was a miracle that we read.
He was saved when all people were against him indeed.
After his conversion, he left off tormenting 'the way.'
Salvation is a miracle, happening many times every day.

Saul's Conversion Experience

Some souls seem to be born gradually into God's Kingdom.
Others seem to be hurled in as headfirst they come.
Some are not sure when exactly it happened to them.
For others, light dawns quickly when they're drawn to Him.

"Who art Thou, Lord?" It's what Saul that day cried.
"I am Jesus whom thou persecutest," the Lord replied.
Saul's world collapsed and his religion was of no use.
The enemy of the gospel was now about to lose.

Saul of Tarsus was the chief of sinners that day.
He wanted to exterminate the church, making them pay.
Saul experienced conversion, in a moment he was changed.
The effects of his mind, heart, and will were all rearranged.

"Lord," Saul said, "What wilt Thou have me to do?"
He now wants to serve the Savior in all ways anew.
He knew in his heart 'faith without works is dead.'
Saul resolved from that day forward to follow God instead.

So, from that day of his conversion, he is well on his way
to become Apostle Paul that we all read of today.
"Born out of due time" is something he would later say.
"But not a whit behind the very chiefest apostles" of the day.

The men who were with him heard the voice, too.
But they saw no one and did not know what to do.
They led Saul (now blind) but he has a new world in view.
He is now converted and will get his sight back anew.

Saul Is Found by Ananias

God told Ananias to go find Saul who is 'now praying.'
Ananias could not believe what God is now saying.
Ananias answered, "I've heard what he has done."
And if he could escape this, he'd set off on the run.

"He hath authority to bind all that call on Your Name."
God said, "He is a chosen vessel unto Me just the same."
Ananias then went and did this thing as he was told.
Addressing him as "Brother Saul," being then so bold.

Saying unto him, "The Lord Jesus who appeared unto thee,
hath sent me to restore thy sight that thou mightiest see."
And immediately as it were, scales fell from his eyes.
He received sight and he arose and was there baptized.

When he received meat, he was strengthened straightway.
He went to the synagogue and began to preach right away.
But all that heard him were amazed at what he now said.
"Isn't this the very same man who wanted us all dead?"

Saying, "This man has come here to destroy us at length."
Still, he made great strides and increased in his strength.
After many days they thought killing him was right.
They watched the gates by both day and by night.

He would now go to Jerusalem and evangelize there.
Surely, they would receive him and show him much care.
There he would join all the other disciples, he assayed.
But they did not receive him because they were afraid.

Saul Becomes Paul

Saul (also called Paul) filled with the Holy Ghost then
is best known as Paul and he stands out among all men.
This name is the one sacred history doth mostly always use.
Paul worked with Greeks and Romans and Peter with the Jews.

'Paul and his company' is what we read from now on.
The name 'Saul' that was used is mostly now gone.
Galatia and the wild regions pull at his heart's string.
He will now go there and the gospel to them bring.

He went to the synagogue the Sabbath day. Sitting down
he read the law and the prophets. The rulers gathered round.
"If you have exhortation for us, say on!" they then said.
Paul stood up and gave history of what he had just read.

He told of Israel's mission and the mistake they did see.
His method assured their interest, and they began to agree.
He started with Israel in Egypt and the blessing God did give.
He brought them to Canaan where they could freely live.

He told them that Israel did the Messiah one day kill.
Then he told them that salvation was eternal and real.
He told them of their ignorance that salvation is at hand.
That God had raised Him and forever He will stand.

Paul then continued, "Be it known unto you therefore,
men and brethren, God has opened for you a door.
Through this Man is preached the forgiveness of sin."
The Gentiles besought Paul, wanting to hear him again.

Paul's First Missionary Journey

When the Jews saw how the Gentiles welcomed Paul's ministry,
they became envious and spoke against his obvious authority.
Paul told them it was necessary to first speak to the Jews.
You would not have any part so this method I must now use.

For so hath the Lord commanded us, I have set thee as a light.
Thou shouldest be to the Gentiles for salvation which is right.
When the Gentiles heard this, they were glad and satisfied.
The Word of God for eternal life, hearing that salvation glorified.

The Jews now rose up and expelled them out of their coasts.
"And the disciples were filled with joy and with the Holy Ghost."
As testimony against them, they shook the dust off their feet.
And they went on to Iconium, a multitude of people to meet.

The people were stirred by unbelieving Jews who divided
and began picking up stones the area around them provided.
But Paul became aware of it and fled unto Lystra and Derbe.
And there preached the gospel, continuing on with his ministry.

Then came certain Jews from Antioch and Iconium one day
saying, "Paul is an impostor and with his life he must pay."
After they had stoned him, then he was placed by the wall
supposing he had been dead, free of him once and for all.

"Howbeit, as the disciples stood round about him, he arose."
They intended to guard his body against all of those.
But what a miracle they witnessed without indication.
And on the next day he went to Derbe, his next destination.

Paul's Second Missionary Journey

Paul confirmed the souls of his disciples and exhorted them, too.
Much tribulation is at hand and by faith they must now continue.
He ordained elders in every church, having prayed with fasting.
Commending them to the Lord that they would boldly be lasting.

And a certain man came down from Judea and began teaching,
"Except ye be circumcised after Moses, the Spirit won't be reaching."
This caused a council to be convened and Peter stood and proclaimed
that Gentiles also had a right to Christ then also to be named.

"And they wrote letters by them after this manner" with a word.
"It seemed good unto us, being assembled with one accord.
To send chosen men unto you, our beloved Barnabas and Paul.
Men that have hazarded their lives for the Lord, giving their all."

And some days later, Paul said to Barnabas, "Let us go there,
visiting each city where we preached and see how they now fare."
Barnabas was determined to take young John Mark, too.
This decision and its contention would separate these two.

And so, Barnabas took Mark and sailed unto Cyprus and, thus,
Paul chose Silas, commended to him, and introduced him to us.
He sought the blessing and prayers of the church that day.
Paul begins his second missionary journey and now sails away.

While confirming the churches, to Derbe and Lystra he came.
"And behold, a certain disciple was there, Timotheus by name."
Because his father was Greek, Paul had to circumcise him.
It was necessary if he wanted to join and go along with them.

Paul's Third Missionary Journey

We find Apostle Paul is no longer on a restful furlough.
Fervent in Spirit, and with the baptism of John he did know.
He started for Galatia and Phrygia and went over them all.
There came a man named Apollos, paying Ephesus a call.

He was welcomed and began to speak boldly to them.
When Aquila and Priscilla had long listened to him,
they took him aside and expounded more perfectly the way.
"Come eat with us, there is a lot more we need to say."

Apollos preached publicly and mightily convinced the Jews.
Showing that Jesus was Christ, by the scriptures he used.
Paul soon came to Ephesus, knowing they had received.
Asking, "Have ye received the Holy Ghost since ye believed?"

They said unto him, "Of the Holy Ghost, we have not heard?"
"Then of what were ye baptized?" "Unto John and his word."
"John verily baptized with the baptism of repentance," he said.
"That you should believe on God's Son, raised from the dead."

When Paul laid hands on them, the Holy Ghost then came.
And they began speaking in tongues and prophesied His Name.
Just as Peter had laid hands on the believers from the start.
Paul was not lacking in anything that the Spirit did impart.

Then Paul went into the synagogue and spoke boldly there.
For the space of three months, he showed them God's care.
He expounded on all things, he was concerned, he persuaded.
But they rejected his message, so he left, other people awaited.

Paul Is A Prisoner

The Jews in Asia saw him in the temple moving about.
Stirred up all the people, laid hands on him, and cried out,
"This man teacheth against people of the law, it is true.
And hath brought Greeks in here polluting me and you."

And all the city moved, then running together and taking
and drew him out to kill him, there'd be no forsaking.
But the chief captain heard the uproar they had made,
took his soldiers and centurions, running in to dissuade.

Demanding of them who was he and why all of this hassle.
With uncertainty, commanded he be brought into the castle.
The chief captain took him, bound in two chains right away.
Some cried out that he must be put to death here today.

The multitude followed after crying, "Away with him, away!"
Paul asked for permission to address them, having his say.
He speaks to them in their own tongue, showing his care.
He gave a long testimony of how it was he got there.

They gave audience to his word, then lifted their voices higher.
They cast off their clothes and they threw dust into the air.
Saying, "Away with him from off the earth; he is not fit to live."
The captain took him inside, so a better answer he could give.

There he bade that he might be examined by scourging then.
They wanted to examine him, but he spoke to the captain of men.
"Is it lawful for you to scourge a man that's Roman?" he asked.
Knowing he's Roman, the chief captain was afraid to do the task.

Paul's Trials As a Prisoner

Paul is accused of sedition and sacrilege and much more.
We see he has confidence, and his conduct is as before.
"But I confess unto thee, that which you now call heresy.
Yet I worship the God of my fathers, and I believe fully."

He said he believed in revelation and the resurrection, too.
He gave them his expression of hope in all he did do.
Telling why he was in the capital; he was sharing his heart.
And telling why they had manipulated him from the start.

We see him before Felix, before Festus, and Agrippa and then,
we could go into each of these hearings from beginning to end.
"To the Jews have I done no wrong, as you well know."
Paul stood his ground and great strength he did show.

Paul gives his testimony again of how God mastered him.
How He revealed His plan that he had shared with them.
How he was given a mission and a message of His plan
about how Christ would suffer for the salvation of man.

Then Agrippa said to Paul, "Almost thou persuadest me
to be a Christian." He side-stepped Paul's effort so easily.
Paul said, "I would to God that not only thou, but also all
who hear me this day, would altogether on Jesus now call."

At the end of Acts, we see Paul dwelling in his own hired place.
Preaching to all who came to him, forbidding no one grace.
Luke's done with church history and finally puts down the pen.
He gave us a picture of Apostle Paul trying to reach all men.

Onesimus

Onesimus was a slave. Worse yet he was on the run.
He belonged body, soul, talent and ability to Philemon.
Philemon is one rare individual that we see among them.
He has a whole book of the Bible written just to him.

We find no reason for Onesimus to have run away.
To be out there all on his own, alone day after day.
Nothing but disaster and death awaited in that line.
His master had been good to him, and he was fine.

All that was expected of him was to simply obey.
It was the one basic all-embracing law of that day.
He was expected to be diligent and loyal to his master.
Fulfilling that law, he could avoid any known disaster.

All he ever needed was there, by his master provided.
Obedience, the sole principle on which life was decided.
And yet he took some possessions and then he fled.
He forsook his master and all of the rules instead.

Philemon was greatly wronged. Onesimus ran away.
He had robbed his master of his good name that day.
Onesimus had a new beginning, new things in mind.
He proclaimed to the world his master was unkind.

By rebellion, Onesimus exposed himself to the full weight
of the law and the wrath that would surely be great.
But Philemon decides to wait and not to pursue.
There is no limit to what a master can decide to do.

Onesimus Is In Danger

Onesimus hated to be told what it was he must do.
He defiantly wanted most to please himself, too.
Why should he obey? Why should he not assert?
If he did what he wanted, who would it hurt?

Why shouldn't he be independent, being his own man?
God didn't make man that way, that wasn't His plan.
Jesus Himself said, "The Father's will must be done."
But Onesimus was a rebel and off then he did run.

The last thing he wants is a master, whom he must obey.
So, he got himself up and shortly thereafter, he ran away.
Wasting no time, he fled as far as he thought necessary.
It mattered not if he had caused his master to worry.

Onesimus is in great danger of being found every day.
He sees the faces of all them who then come his way.
This bothered him and caused him very much dread.
He hated the thoughts of ever going back instead.

Runaway slaves, when caught, were then crucified.
He lived with a great fear of death, causing him to hide.
If there was a way out, he would openly choose it.
Death certainly had his scent and would never lose it.

Such was Onesimus' condition, he was in great danger.
He was outside of Christ and to salvation a stranger.
This story of Onesimus rings for us ever so true.
What is it that this fugitive from justice can do?

Onesimus's Dramatic Conversion

He is a fugitive from justice and a stranger to grace.
Lost in a far country having to daily hide his face.
And there, salvation overtook him. We find
it was the last thing that he had on his mind.

His only hope was that he could make it on his own
and avoid the wrath he'd earned by being gone.
Then one day he was arrested, not by lawful men.
He had an encounter with Paul who knew his sin.

Salvation overtook him; he'd fled fast and far.
But salvation will find you wherever you are.
There will come a time, there will come a place.
Although the details may be different in every case.

Paul knew Philemon and Paul knew of his loss.
He must have brought Onesimus quickly to the cross.
It is not recorded what happened to him that day.
But we see Onesimus was then changed right away.

Down go the arms of his rebellion right then.
As a slave, he is convinced to give up his sin.
He gives in to Jesus and lays aside all his strife.
And his name is written in the Lamb's Book of Life.

Salvation brought Onesimus into a new world that day.
He was overwhelmed that it could be this way.
Salvation purchases for us not only eternal life we know
but a new dimension of life as forward we now go.

Onesimus Must Go Home

"And now Onesimus," says Paul, "you must return home again.
Back to Philemon and the place you were back then."
Salvation cancels our debt to God but before very long,
he has a quickened conscience about what's right and wrong.

Onesimus belonged to Philemon, so back he must go.
And he had stolen some money, there's no way to escape so,
he must go back and throw himself on the mercy of the man
and convince Philemon he's now following a different plan.

He is a new man in Christ and if his life is now spared,
he will be the most eager slave Philemon has desired.
If Philemon demanded punishment, it wouldn't be good.
And Apostle Paul did not think that his master would.

So, Paul wrote a letter for him to take with him that day.
As mediator he'd stand between them to smooth the way.
As to the debt he's accrued, "Put that on my account.
Impute it to me, I will repay," whatever the amount

Just as our Redeemer takes our debt and our shame
and charges it to His account if we but trust in His Name.
"Receive him back forever," Paul now writes as a plea.
The same relationship exists between Onesimus and me.

If you count me as a partner, receive him now, I plea.
He is a new man in Christ and very soon you will see.
We are sons of God, joint heirs with Jesus and one day
we will be seated with Him in heavenly places to stay.

Simon The Sorcerer

The Samaritans had been slighted and scorned by the Jew.
There was a great gulf fixed between these two.
Neither one was willing to accept the other then.
They fought like dogs and cats and not as disgruntled men.

But the whole city of Samaria was stirred one day
when Philip came forth preaching, "Christ is the way."
A deacon of the Jerusalem church and he reminded them
that Jesus Christ died for all and now draws all to Him.

For even them too, as a sacrifice on Calvary, He did die.
And is now seated at the right hand of the Majesty on high.
He gave out the good news that Jesus was willing to save.
And revival broke out due to the gospel he then gave.

Heaven's man was in town, but hell's man was there, too.
He called himself Simon Magnus, 'the magician' to you.
He watched Philip very closely and with greedy eyes.
For he was a sorcerer, but he kept hidden his despise.

Simon often used sorcery to keep town people fooled.
He didn't want them to know it was Jesus who ruled.
He had them all thinking he was some kind of great man.
And he "bewitched" them into following his plan.

He was overwhelmed by the miracles Philip did perform.
His ability to do those was beyond Simon's norm.
Being an imposter, the Devil's man-made profession.
Maybe now he, too, will have the Holy Ghost possession.

Simon Performs Magic

There seems to be little doubt that Simon can perform
things that are not considered to be of the norm.
He was a practitioner of the black arts, and we see he can
do extraordinary things by the mystery and magic of Satan.

We do not know if he did all the things he would relate.
He did beyond the capabilities of people in a normal state.
Satan has great power, and he confers power to those
who will dedicate themselves to him, as everyone knows.

Simon had practiced his craft and he had Samaria in thrall.
Then came forth Philip, answering the Holy Spirit's call.
Simon and his magic sorcery very soon then has paled.
The Devil, with his wiles, against the Holy Spirit then failed.

Philip was filled with the Holy Ghost from the first hour.
Simon pondered the evangelist's preaching and power.
Simon heard the truth with conviction and concern.
He listened closely, thinking maybe he could learn.

Simon heard the truth, and he did that day surmise
that all of his life he had been wrapped up in lies.
He was both a deceiver and he had been deceived, too.
He worked hand in glove with Satan in all he did do.

Straight to the point was the preaching he did face.
He heard about God's sovereignty and about His grace.
If he wanted this day to be by the Lord now employed,
he would have to give up everything he now enjoyed.

Simon Perceived a Miracle

It wasn't long before Peter and John soon came to town.
They had been acquaintances of Jesus and men of renown.
Simon saw that Philip gave them much attention and love.
These two men were exceptional, they were a cut above.

Simon watched eagerly what Peter and John would do.
He did not have to wait long for action by these two.
They prayed and laid hands on those who had believed.
And the gift of the Holy Ghost was then by them received.

It made a profound impression on Simon Magnus indeed.
He decided that power was something that he did need.
He needed that power; we can almost hear his thought.
He'd get the Holy Ghost power even if it had to be bought.

Satan does not yield possession of such an excellent tool.
Simon knew if he had the power, he would have to fool.
So, Simon Magnus then met Simon Peter face to face.
He went straight to his point, much to his disgrace.

"Give me also this power, that on whomsoever I lay hands,
may receive the Holy Ghost." He had some great plans.
"Thy money perish with thee because thou hast thought
the gift of God may be purchased and with money bought."

Simon had deceived Philip but he couldn't deceive these two.
Frightened by Peter's words, he knew what he must do.
"Let not these things come upon me, I hereby implore."
Simon's heart was yet as rotten as it had been before.

Luke the Doctor

We owe a lot to this great, gifted, and good man
who stays in the background as much as he can.
But he did write two books that are included herein.
We know him simply as Luke, a man among men.

His name is mentioned only three times as we see.
But we read, he often included the little word 'we'.
He was Paul's personal physician, traveling with him.
And at times things became difficult and very dim.

We know him best as a historian who did write
and told us that everything would one day be alright.
Others left Paul when he was imprisoned, he said,
but Luke stayed with him, caring for him instead.

Luke asked people who witnessed Jesus' ministry so bold.
And he recorded the things from what they had told.
A lot of the parables that were recorded, we know
would not be mentioned if Luke had not told us so.

Luke tells of six miracles that no one else mentioned.
He had a great vocabulary that draws our attention.
Throughout his writing, we see the influence of Paul.
He emphasizes faith and the repentance for us all.

Luke is fond of the words grace, salvation, and Savior.
His gospel illustrates Paul's concepts and behavior.
The two books he has written for us to now read
will help us greatly if we but read them and heed.

Luke the Helper

Luke traveled with Paul to aide, making sure of no lack.
Constantly attending to his much-lacerated back.
Paul had what he called his "thorn in the flesh" then.
He would not give up; he must preach to more men.

With all the hardships, shipwrecks, and scourgings, there
is little wonder Paul needed constant physician care.
Dr. Luke was most always at hand so he could
do whatever Paul needed to make him feel good.

When we read of that long list of perils he endured,
it is remarkable that Luke could keep him cured.
And go on to the next obstacle that stood in the way.
Knowing that the end would soon come his way one day.

Paul was again imprisoned and constantly he's chained.
There he spent the rest of his life that remained.
He was friendless and forsaken, and often he was cold.
But Luke stuck by him, Luke was so very bold.

They often brought him things he had asked for
but they would quickly leave and not stay anymore.
It's a good thing he had Luke as his number one friend
who wrote this all down, right to the very end.

Luke remained with the aged apostle that day
until he was taken by the executioner and led away.
His head was struck from his body and then his soul
soared upward to heaven; which was his goal.

Demas

Demas means "of the people" or as we would say
"one of the crowd" or "popular" as we use it today.
Three times in the New Testament we read about him.
Each time he is mentioned, he is different from them.

Paul calls Demas a "fellow laborer" in his brief memo.
Paul is under house arrest at this time as we all know.
Demas is one on which Paul depends to get things done.
He's with Paul, doing things Paul wishes, always on a run.

Demas was at this time a very diligent man we read.
He wanted to spread the gospel to all who would heed.
We first see him as a persistent man who was not afraid.
He was Paul's hands and feet and close to him he stayed.

He was an assistant to Paul yet he had some dire lack.
He would go and accomplish and then come right back.
Nero was now in charge and he persecuted the church.
Soon we learn Demas would leave Paul in a dire lurch.

When we first saw Demas he was a diligent man.
He was brought to the front assisting a great man.
But now we see him as he has fast slipped away.
And in the world he does his own thing today.

Paul wrote, "Demas has forsaken me." Oh, what a shame.
"Having loved this present world," is now his claim.
There is not much detail in the New Testament abiding.
Today we associate "Demas" with Christian "backsliding."

Antichrist

He has lots of names by which he is often called.
He will come one day and leave the earth appalled.
He has been foreshadowed in history time and again
by many a man who negatively affected other men.

He was thwarted in his effort to destroy the man-child,
the Lord Jesus at His birth, the One meek and mild.
He is the scarlet-colored beast, a fact as we all know.
He acts like the great red dragon wherever he doth go.

There is much written of him, too numerous to mention.
His number one goal will be to get man's attention.
The False Prophet will persuade men the Antichrist is savior.
He will try his best to convince them to be in his favor.

The Antichrist will sign a treaty with Israel and then,
when they've finished the temple, he'll turn on all men.
He will show them he has only for them much disgrace.
He will tear off his mask and now show them his face.

Under no circumstance will God abdicate His throne.
He knows what the Antichrist is doing and what's going on.
He will not for a moment surrender His sovereignty.
The antichrist's day of reckoning will come quickly.

The judgment of the Antichrist and False Prophet is sure.
They will be flung headlong into the lake of fire to endure.
The 'sheep' from the 'goats' will have all been cleared.
The new millennial kingdom of Christ will have appeared.

More Books by Elvis "Raz" Stephens

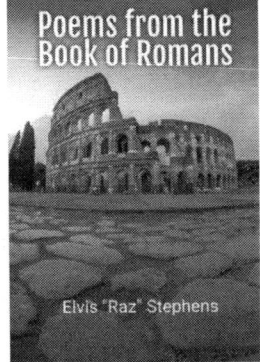

Made in the USA
Middletown, DE
23 June 2023

32975265R00088

Made in the USA
Middletown, DE
23 June 2023